Masonic Perspectives:
The Thoughts of a Grand Secretary

Also from Plumbstone

Sing the Art Divine:
A Traditional Masonic Songster
Nathan St. Pierre *&* Shawn Eyer

Ahiman: A Review of Masonic Culture & Tradition
Shawn Eyer, Editor

The Meaning of Masonry
Walter Leslie Wilmshurst

The Masonic Initiation
Walter Leslie Wilmshurst

Masonic Perspectives

THE THOUGHTS OF
A GRAND SECRETARY

Thomas W. Jackson

Plumbstone
WASHINGTON, D.C.

Chapters 1 through 40 of this anthology were
originally published in *The Pennsylvania Freemason.*

Cover painting copyright © 2015 by Ryan J. Flynn.
Prints available at *http://www.ryanjflynn.com.*

Publisher's Cataloging-in-Publication data
Jackson, Thomas William, 1934–
      Masonic perspectives: the thoughts of a grand
      secretary / Thomas W. Jackson
      122 p. 23 cm.
      ISBN-13 978-1-60302-020-6 (paperback)
      ISBN-13 978-1-60302-021-3 (e-book)
      1. Freemasons. 2. Freemasonry—United States.
      I. Title

Library of Congress Control Number: 2015947837

http://www.plumbstone.com

This book is dedicated to the memory of
Brother Samuel (Wally) Harper,
one of my greatest friends in life,
who said to me over 52 years ago,
"Tom, you should be a Freemason."
A man who truly knew and practiced
the Brotherhood of Man.
A Prince Hall Freemason.

[Contents]

[Preface]

Several years ago, I began, at the urgings of many of my friends, compiling my writings and addresses into book form. I soon recognized the logic in separating my articles from *The Pennsylvania Freemason* into a separate, smaller publication.

Although I was elected to the position of Right Worshipful Grand Secretary in December of 1979, I did not begin writing articles for *The Pennsylvania Freemason* until May of 1988.

The articles found here are in the same order as they were published in *The Pennsylvania Freemason*. Several articles were not included in this anthology because they related only to Pennsylvania Freemasons.

This small book also includes several addresses that I gave which were unrelated to Freemasonry. I include them so that you might garner a better understanding of the personality I acquired through my commitment to Freemasonry and the Boy Scouts of America.

In rereading these articles, I found that some of my thinking has changed over the years, and I might have phrased some of my comments differently. Nonetheless, my overall philosophy regarding Freemasonry has not changed. Where I was once a consummate idealist, I have found that my idealism has been tempered in the flames of reality. As a result, much of my early thinking and writings tended to concentrate upon the subject of how great the Fraternity was. Now, I tend to write and speak more frequently on my concern over our losing that greatness. While I will always remain an idealist, I now regard myself as a pragmatic idealist.

[1]

Well Said!

On February 17, 1825, Silentia Lodge N⁰ 198 was constituted in Shippensburg, Pennsylvania, but went out of existence on February 6, 1837.

On February 18, 1858, Cumberland Valley Lodge N⁰ 315 was constituted in Shippensburg. The warrant master at that time was Brother Henry Ruby, Sr., and his remarks on assuming the duties as Worshipful Master of the Lodge are worthy of note.

> In assuming the honorable and elevated position as Worshipful Master of this Lodge, I cannot forbear thanking you for the part taken in having me invested with the Constitutional Authority of the Right Worshipful Grand Lodge by which this Lodge is to be directed in her labors and good government.
>
> Among the many honorable positions I've been favored with in public life, I regard this one as among the least merited, but the most exalted in my history. From my inexperience, and the important labors I am called to perform as Master, I would be violating my feelings, did I not give utterance in this connection, to my fears and not fully realizing your expectations.
>
> But in casting eyes around me and seeing myself encircled with brethren good and true, I take courage in going forward in the discharge of the duties of my

office, and in so doing, I shall strive to perform them to the best of my ability.

With a view of accomplishing successfully the work before us as a Lodge in accordance with the ancient landmarks of the Craft, I shall look to you, my brethren in office in the West and in the South, on my right and on my left, for counsel and aid.

Thus united in our effort, I feel assured we will be able to prove ourselves worthy of the confidence that the Right Worshipful Grand Lodge has been pleased to commit into our hands. And, my brethren, when done with carrying out the designs drawn by the Sovereign Architect of the Universe upon the spiritual trestle board of our earthly existence, may we all be well prepared to enter the door of mercy of our Great Divine Master, into those mansions beyond the skies, where love and peace, and joy forever reign.

[2]

A National Grand Lodge

I have become more aware through numerous inquiries since I have been in the office of Grand Secretary that many of our members are unaware that there is no national level Masonic organization for Craft Freemasonry. Each state and the District of Columbia (with the exception of Hawaii, which operates under the Grand Lodge of California) operates its own Grand Jurisdiction and is autonomous in its own right. This is also true of the provinces of Canada other than Newfoundland.

There was a proposal offered in 1779, that Brother George Washington be made General Grand Master of the United States. (It is interesting to note that the Grand Lodge of Pennsylvania supported this proposal.) The proposal, however, was never adopted. There has never been a National Grand Lodge of the United States of America. There are, however, a number of national Masonic organizations supported by the Grand Lodges which function for the benefit of Freemasonry in general. Two with which you are probably most familiar are the George Washington Masonic National Memorial Association and the Masonic Service Association.

The George Washington Masonic National Memorial Association is responsible for the maintenance and operation of the George Washington Masonic National Memorial, an imposing structure which sits on Shuters Hill in Alexandria, Virginia. It is the only national Masonic memorial in the United States, and was dedicated to the memory of Brother George Washington in the year 1932. The annual maintenance and operating costs of this Memorial range between $700,000 and $1,000,000.

The Masonic Service Association, was organized in 1919 and has a multifaceted function. The Association serves as an educational and informational organization by publishing and producing a variety of bulletins, digests, newsletters, statistical information films and audio tapes.

It also serves as a clearinghouse of factual information concerning the Fraternity. The Association, in addition, is responsible for investigating and issuing appeals to Masonic Bodies for the relief of human needs of Masons and their families resulting from disasters and catastrophes. The operating cost for this phase of the organization is $250,000 a year, which is supported by subscription rates for publications such as the *Short Talk Bulletin* and contributions from members.

The second major function of the Association is the operation the Hospital Visitation Program. The Hospital Visitation Program operates for the purpose of providing personal services in more than 140 Veterans Administration Medical Centers, Veterans Homes and Military Hospitals. The budget for this program in 1988 was $353,000 and is solely supported by contributions from the Masonic fraternity.

This program depends not only upon financial support, but also the contribution of time of our members as Hospital Visitation Field Agents. These brethren contribute more than one-half million volunteer hours of service each year. Pennsylvania presently is in need of volunteers in three locations: the Veterans Hospital in Coatesville; the Veterans Administration Medical Center in Pittsburgh, Aspinwall

4

division; and the Veterans' Hospital in Philadelphia. Any brother willing to provide this badly needed service, please contact my office.

[3]

He Also Lived As a Freemason

The headlines on the front page of a small-town newspaper recently declared, "Roy Griffith Died While Helping Others."The article accompanying the headline told the story of a man of admirable quality who lost his life in serving others.

It did not mention it in the article, but the man was a member of the Masonic Fraternity, and herein lies what could be and should be a story of Freemasonry.

Brother Roy Griffith, 74 years of age, died of injuries received in a traffic accident while he and his wife of forty-seven years were delivering Meals on Wheels, a project he was involved with for more than 10 years. His wife was very seriously injured. "He is the only person to die in the history of Meals on Wheels, while delivering meals."

Brother Griffith's life, according to the article, reflects those principles which should ever characterize the members of our order. Quoting from the article, "He was a man of conviction who got things done. He was a kind of person who believed that if you could not act out your Christian faith, you did not have Christian faith."

He was president of the trustees of his church, as well as an Elder and a Deacon. Brother Griffith had not missed a day of Sunday school in forty-four years while his wife had sixty years of perfect attendance, excluding a period during World War II, when she worked Sundays at an Army Depot.

It is regrettable that the article failed to refer to his Masonic affiliation, but I would like to think that either Masonry contributed toward those higher qualities he possessed, or that the higher qualities of Freemasonry attracted him to it.

Men of the quality and character of Brother Roy Griffith will do more to promote the future Freemasonry than all the praise we may seek and receive, all the credits we may search out and have heaped upon us, or all of the glory of our past in which we bask.

I am certain that there are hundreds, even thousands of Roy Griffiths, comprising the Masonic fraternity, each making no great mark on the world, but in their own way of leaving some positive mark. The newspaper article concluded, "He was a doer, not a talker." Brother Griffith may not have been heralded outside of his own community, but he lived a life that resulted in headline news on the front page of the local newspaper. Few of us, no matter how great we think we are, will achieve as much.

[4]

A Brotherhood of Man
under the Fatherhood of God

One of the most frequently asked questions I receive is, "What is Freemasonry?" You would think that for someone in my position this question would have an easy answer, but after all these years, I still find it difficult to come up with an explanation that can be understood by everyone.

We have many beautiful sounding words and phrases which we use to define the Fraternity, but tend to leave the questioner unfulfilled, such as, "a beautiful system of morality veiled in allegory and illustrated by symbols." The simplest and perhaps the most meaningful definition, however, is: "Freemasonry is a brotherhood of Man under the Fatherhood of God."

A second frequently asked question is how we are any different from other fraternal organizations. Other than obvious differences, such as the social structure and the beneficent character of these organizations our promotion of the Brotherhood of Man with the belief in God as a foundation stands forth with uniqueness.

I suspect that a major cause of the lack of interest today by many members of society in our great Fraternity is that the feeling of brotherhood is not nearly as strong as it was in the past. Freemasonry evolved from the operative to the speculative and hence, the fraternity of the practitioner to a fraternity of the idealist. It was the strength of these ideals which caused Freemasonry, to become the greatest fraternity in the world.

Our modern way of life has regretfully, deprived Freemasonry of the opportunity of doing many of those personal brotherly acts which cemented us to work together in the past.

Masons today, and especially our younger brothers, have not had the opportunity to experience this quality of Brotherhood nor the feeling of satisfaction which accompanies it.

We must strive to regain our stature, of former years, to move Freemasonry outside the lodge room and again make it the constructive influence in the lives of the community. We must re-emphasize this basic tenet of Freemasonry. Then, indeed, we will be a Brotherhood of Man under the Fatherhood of God.

[5]

The Lodge Secretary

Back in 1969 when I was Worshipful Master of my Lodge, I went through twelve months in which I really thought I was an excellent Master. It was only after I was out of the line for a period of time that I realized my assumed greatness was due to having a great secretary. I have since had the privilege to preside over twelve Masonic bodies and I've really learned the value of a good secretary.

During my term as Grand Secretary, I have developed an even greater appreciation for the value of a "good" Lodge Secretary. My definition of a "good" Lodge Secretary is: "He is the man who runs the Lodge, and lets the Worshipful Master think he's doing it." *He is the one continuity from one Master to the next and for that reason has the accumulated knowledge to guide them.* It is my absolute opinion that today the most vital hope for the success of our Fraternity is the Subordinate Lodge Secretary. He is the link between his Lodge and the members of his Lodge with the Grand Lodge.

Regretfully, in the ten years that I served in the office of Grand Secretary, I have watched more and more of our good secretaries retiring or leaving the office. Unfortunately, many of our lodges today are filling the chair of office of secretary with someone who has little interest in doing an efficient job.

This, the most vital of Masonic offices, is also many

times, one of the most thankless in the recognition of a job well done. All too often, lodges, simply expect a good job without consideration of the effort required. The greatest reward that a secretary receives is an intangible—it is the knowledge of the great benefit he has provided his Lodge and the Masonic Fraternity.

My brethren, your Lodge greatly needs those of you with the competence, willingness and dedication to serve as Secretary. Please, if you have never considered this office, give it some thought. We are here today because of brethren of the past, and it now becomes our inherent obligation to provide the continuity for continuance to a future. Our brethren of the past did not fail us; let it never be said that we failed brethren of the future.

[6]

The Penalties of the Obligations

In 1985, a change in our ritual was issued providing for the removal of the penalties from the obligation and their relocation within the ritual. This change probably created a greater expression of opinion, both pro and con, than any other change in Pennsylvania Freemasonry.

I use this column not to express my opinion, but rather to express some of the rationale of prominent Masonic personages regarding the penalties and their significance to our Fraternity.

In 1969, the Grand Lodge of Pennsylvania reduced the significance of the penalties by qualifying their symbolic presence in the obligations. Some members felt that the removal from the obligation of the penalties was due to outside influences rather than to rational thought. There was, however, much internal dissension voiced within the fraternity, long before outside opinions were addressed. Others looked at the change as a divergence from the landmarks. The ritual, however, is not a landmark and never has been regarded as such.

In 1964, the United Grand Lodge of England instituted what many members thought was an "unsatisfactory compromise" following an evaluation at their Quarterly by Brother Bishop Herbert. At a quarterly communication, the Most Worshipful Grand Master stated:

In such a serious matter as an obligation, it must be considered whether the penalties included are really meant or not. Clearly they could not be, and never could have been actually enforced even 250 years ago. If therefore, the penalties in the obligation are not really meant, this must throw doubt on whether the obligation is binding so far as the other, more important, matters it contains are concerned.

The most logical rebuttal to critics opposing the change is that we were requiring our members to obligate themselves on the Volume of the Sacred Law to penalties which violated some of our very principles. After qualifying the penalties as symbolic, we then obligated them to a meaningless series of words. The explanation of the signs now lies outside the obligation, and they are not decreed as meaningless, but rather as an integral part of our history.

At another Quarterly Communication of the United Grand Lodge of England Very Worshipful Brother Maj-Gen. Denis A. Beckett expressed what may well be the foremost logical thinking for consideration of the change when he stated, "Brethren, Freemasonry does not exist in a vacuum; it is woven into the fabric of the society in which we live and have our being. If it is to continue to exercise its beneficial influence and to continue to attract candidates able and willing to serve its ideals it must be sensitive to changes taking place in society whilst standing firm on the grand principles on which it is founded. What was acceptable in days gone by, is not always acceptable today and maybe even less so tomorrow."

No change is ever going to satisfy all members of any organization, but it is necessary in the evolution of an organization to resist stagnation. When resistance requires change, it is then the responsibility the leadership to make the change.

I again emphasize that I am not necessarily expressing my opinion. However, changes have been instituted. Change for the sake of change will never serve a viable purpose, but refusal to make a change when deemed necessary, is dooming any organization to extinction. This decision was based upon an analysis of some of the greatest minds in Freemasonry.

Individually, we may not always agree, on changes that take place within our Fraternity. It is, however, important for us to recognize that when changes do take place our acceptance and support is necessary to maintain our strength. Freemasonry, has always been and always will be greater than any of its component parts. Individuals have come and gone, and will continue to come and go, and in my opinion, or the opinion of any other individual, will have no great lasting effect on it.

[7]

Of Which Are You a Part?

"I do not think you know my husband can't walk for six years. I am 81 years old and take care of him and also teach music for food money. He is very lonesome, could you send someone to talk with him?"

"I am sorry but my husband is in a nursing home with Alzheimer's disease since 1987. He never got as much as a card for any of his friends in your organization."

"My husband has been in a nursing home for 19 months, he cannot walk. Is very hard for me to keep a smile. Please send him a card. It may make him feel good."

"My father's been in a nursing home since 1987. As a member of all branches of the Masons (listed), I am sorry and sad to inform you that my father has been totally forgotten. Not one card has he received. He was in the clown unit and donated generously. Now, isn't it a shame that a 25-cent postage stamp can't be used to make his day a bit nicer?"

My brethren, these are excerpts from letters received by our R.W. Grand Master in response to our charitable appeal. Isn't it sad? Perhaps it spells out clearly why we have difficulty today in attracting new members. Perhaps it is a delineating factor which separates us from Freemasonry of the past. Were we to analyze our responsibility to our brethren as exemplified in the past versus today, it might be all we would need to define our problems and obtain our answers.

"My former employee pays me a small pension. My spouse receives no pension. A small Social Security payment is her only income. Circumstances and future doesn't look promising. My wife requires expensive medications. Enclosed is $50 to help in operating the hospital at the homes. We know you need help."

This is also a response from the same appeal, and perhaps reveals much of that which is good in our fraternity. In the worst of times, there are those amongst us who think of others. Two types of responses: one exposing a weakness, the other a strength. Which do you want to look upon yourself as being a part?

My Brothers, never forget, someday we might be lying in a nursing home and would want nothing more than a card or a visit from a Brother to brighten our day. In brightening the day of a brother, we could very well be brightening our future.

"There is a destiny that makes us brothers.
None goes his way alone.
All that we send into the lives of others
Comes back into ours."
Brother Edwin Markham

[8]

Preparation for Our Future

For generations, our members have been pointing with pride to the greatness of our fraternity, and justifiably so. Disregarding the influence in any way of any religion, there has probably been no organization ever conceived by the mind of man that has created more reason for pride than has Freemasonry. None has the potential to do so much good. None has a comparable philosophy developed for the absolute promotion of the brotherhood of man. None encourages any more vigorously the devotion in support of their faith and their country.

However, it has been our inclination to point more to members who have been known for their greatness and not nearly enough to the greatness of the organization itself.

There have been many great men who have been Masons and again, we have been justifiably proud that we attract great men, but there is a difference between great men who have been Masons and great Masons. Great men who are Masons are a noted asset but great Masons, are our future. Great men who have been Masons are counted in thousands. Great men who are also great Masons are counted in hundreds.

As a result of this inclination, we have a tendency to lose sight of the need for quality leadership within the fraternity. There is nothing wrong with being proud of our past, unless, in so doing, we ignore the present upon which we must base our future. We must stop looking back, if it is going to interfere with looking forward. We cannot afford to ignore the future for we must spend the rest of our lives there, and what we do today totally determines the quality of that future.

Preparation for the future must include more than expressing lovely platitudes and referring to ancient accomplishments. We cannot assume that Freemasonry, because it is so old, is eternal. Nor can we afford to assume the leadership will always be provided by others.

We, my brethren, are the only internal variable of Freemasonry, and if we become less than what we are, we must shoulder the responsibility for that regression.

Undoubtably, we have all permitted ourselves to bask in the knowledge that so many great names eternally recorded in the annals of history have been Freemasons. We must also, however, recognize that for future generations to have the same privilege, we need the contribution of those with the capability of becoming great Masons. Greatness is a quality earned, not a quality passively acquired or passively maintained.

Each one of us, when we knelt before the altar, and assumed our obligations, became not only a member of the Craft, but also assumed the responsibility to preserve that Craft, not necessarily in the phraseology of the obligation, but in the acknowledgment of the privilege granted us.

Freemasonry, has become the end product to some of the greatest thinkers of the ages. We must be egotistical enough to recognize that the world needs us. The future of Freemasonry lies now in our hands. I would hope that it can never be said sometime in the distant future that our fraternity failed due to the lack of contributions of leadership in our time.

[9]

We Have Made Masonic Membership
Too Easily Obtainable

While at the Conference of Grand Secretaries recently, I had the opportunity to be with Grand officers from the newly reorganized Grand Lodges of Yugoslavia and Czechoslovakia. I was impressed with the impact Freemasonry had upon these men. The genuine expression of brotherly love was very evident. It has been many years since Eastern Block residents had the privilege of Masonic membership. It is significant that Freemasonry has become one of the first organizations to be re-established upon shedding the mantle of dictatorial Communism. Hungary has also had a re-organization of its Grand Lodge.

This experience has caused me to coalesce some thoughts and concerns which have been troubling me for years. Mainly, why do so many members in the United States fail to place the importance on Freemasonry that is found in so many other jurisdictions?

For more than eleven years, I have been in communication with probably all the recognized grand lodges in the world and have found the appreciation of the fraternity to be much greater in most foreign jurisdictions than in our own country. It should be worth our while to try to determine why.

The basic precepts and philosophy, the fundamentals

of the ritual and the "Ancient Landmarks" are a relative constant throughout the world. The difference, therefore, must lie in the composition of, and attitudes generated by our membership.

We live in a society today that equates value with cost and desirability with the degree of difficulty to obtain. Have you ever wondered why very expensive private clubs have waiting lists? Consider your own system of placing an item's value on its relationship to cost. How many of us purchase the cheapest priced item available in the category in which we are considering? I know that when I am looking to purchase, I assume the more expensive item to be of better quality.

I am convinced that we have created Freemasonry's greatest problem by making it too easily obtainable and too cheaply retainable.

For jurisdictions in the United States, the financial cost to become a member and the dues to remain a member are considerably less than most other Grand Jurisdictions. In most, annual dues are many times higher than those of any Lodge in our jurisdiction. The cost to affiliate with the fraternity, in many, represents a large percentage of the petitioner's annual salary.

In addition, in many Grand Jurisdictions if you miss a stated meeting you are required to write in advance, giving justifiable cause. Failure to do so can result in suspension. I recently received a Lodge Notice from St. Oswald Lodge number 4260 in Darlington, England, and I quote from this notice: "from ancient times, no Master or Fellow could be absent from his Lodge, especially when warned to appear at it, without inviting a severe censure, unless it appeared to the Master and Wardens that pure necessity hindered him."

For many years. We've heard it stated that we have

"sold" Freemasonry, too cheaply. Our greatest concern seems to be to make Freemasonry readily accessible to anyone who wishes to say "I am a Freemason." It is my evaluation that the result has been that far too many of our members take their membership for granted, and this fact alone has undeniably caused a decline in the prestige of Masonic membership. Lack of interest must be directly related to lack of assumed value, and lack of value to lack of what we expect and require.

To reverse this trend, we should take a serious look at how easy we have made it to be a Freemason, and give some serious consideration as to whether this is the pathway we wish to continue to follow. Our decision may well determine our future.

[10]

Response to Anti-Masonic Criticism

One of the most frequent requests I receive is to provide a response that members can give to those who speak out against Freemasonry, especially to those who represent "the Church." In recent years, our members have become more aware of anti-Masonic propaganda, not only because of the increase of radical attitudes within various religious groups, but also because of the use of modern media for them to disseminate their message.

Most of our members when they hear or see this propaganda, become very defensive and wish to respond to it. We have, however, lost very few members as a result of it.

There is little value for the average member of the Masonic fraternity to attempt to debate these radical elements of the church. In most cases their minds are closed to any but their own ideas.

The Duke of Kent, in an address to the United Grand Lodge of England, stated that "many of us become Freemasons because we know that someone whom we admire is both in the Craft and proud of it." I doubt very much if we consider the reason we became a member of the Masonic Fraternity, whether there has been a change in that reason.

I'm not aware of any organized religion other than some elements of the Christianity that take specific issue with the fraternity. Yet, some of the most notable men who have ever lived have been both Freemason and Christian. The radical elements of Christianity infer that none can be both, and imply since Freemasonry is not a Christian organization, it must be anti-Christ. Knowing what we know, this form of reasoning is so totally irrational. Think back; when have you ever heard of any anti-religious comments of any kind in Freemasonry?

I would ask these critics of Freemasonry how many men like Dr. Norman Vincent Peale, Dr. Joseph Fort Newton and Dr. Albert Schweitzer (as per the Grand Lodge of Gabon), great Christian leaders, could justify their membership. The implication that they were either ignorant of the true meaning of Freemasonry or were not true Christians is an impossible assumption.

Writings by some of our own members are quoted as evidence of a reason to oppose it. Remember that what is written by a Freemason does not necessarily reflect Freemasonry's philosophy, any more than all ministers' writings reflect the philosophy of the Church.

All members of the Fraternity will probably at one time or another be exposed to anti-Masonic propaganda. It is advantageous for each of us to be able to discuss intelligently our relationship with our God, and our Craft. It is recommended, however, that debate be left to those qualified to debate. Do not allow yourself to become antagonistic or overly defensive. Freemasonry, due to its inherent truths and principles, has survived far greater threats than these. The best defense we can offer is by living lives which exemplify the true meaning of Freemasonry. We then will be the example to someone who wishes to join because of those he admires within the Craft.

Recommended reading: "A Factual View of Freemasonry" by Rev. Bishop Fred P. Corson, Grand Chaplain, *The Pennsylvania Freemason*, February 1965; "Freemasons and

Organized Religion" by Rev. Dr. Charles H. Lacquement, Grand Chaplain, *The Pennsylvania Freemason*, February 1989; "Freemasonry and Religion," by the Supreme Council, A.A.S.R., Southern Jurisdiction.

[11]

The Obligation We Assumed

Freemasonry, a Brotherhood of Man under the Father-hood of God, is perhaps our greatest and simplest definition, yet one whose precept we frequently fail to practice, and I would suspect one that many of our brothers fail to appreciate or even comprehend. I use this column to relate an experience I had which I think describes what might be the essence of Freemasonry, at least to, the individual member.

One Saturday afternoon, after working in my garden, I went indoors to lie on the bed and listen to a Penn State football game. The telephone rang, and the caller was a representative of the Western Aid Society, calling from Texas. She told me that a young lady was on an airplane scheduled to land at the Philadelphia airport in one hour. Her sister, who lived in New Jersey, had been injured in an automobile accident, and she was arriving to take her home to Texas. She knew no one to contact and had no way to get to New Jersey. The only thing she could tell a Women's Aid Society was that, "her daddy was a Mason."

This lady called the Grand Lodge of Texas, who referred her to my office. One of the employees who happened to be in the office on Saturday gave her my home telephone number.

I went to the airport and after a two-hour search was able to locate the girl. I learned from a Brother Mason, who was a security officer how to get to the small town in New Jersey. On the way there, the girl told me that she needed to rent a truck to carry her sister's furniture and clothing to Texas. They wanted to leave the next day.

Upon arriving at the location in New Jersey, I was unable to contact the local Lodge or the Grand Secretary of New Jersey. I was also unable to rent a truck that late at night.

Being close to the Delaware border, I called the Grand Secretary of Delaware at his home. He, in turn, made arrangements for four members of one of Delaware's Lodges to come over Sunday morning, rent a truck, load it and get the girls started for Texas. I stayed until 3 a.m. helping them pack their belongings in boxes which I was able to obtain from a local store.

It is not significant that I was involved or, for that matter, that any single person was involved in this episode. The individual is not important.

What is important is our feeling of the need to respond due to a Masonic obligation. What is important is that five words, "my daddy was a Mason," given to a non-Masonic organization in Texas precipitated a response that involved four states across a continent. What is important is that it reveals the continuing essence of Freemasonry. "The Brotherhood of Man."

As long as we, as individual members, feel the need to respond to this assumed obligation, we carry on the proud tradition credited to the Craft. We justify our existence. We give reason for an interest by others. We really maintain a reason for being. If each brother would express and respond to this motivation to practice this "essence"—what a giant step for our survival!

[12]

The Dedication of a Brother

I'm using my column in this issue to tell two stories which need to be told. For over twelve years I've been listening to the difficulties in presenting Fifty-Year Masonic Service Emblems, to brothers who did not wish to make the effort to travel a few miles of even a few blocks to receive the award.

Several years ago, I received a request from a good friend and brother to present him with his Fifty-Year Masonic Service Emblem when he was eligible to receive it. With permission of the District Deputy Grand Master for his district, I readily accepted what I regarded as a rare privilege and an honor.

Last year I had the opportunity to make that presentation. My friend and brother boarded a bus in Sedalia, Missouri (where he now lives) and travel to Lebanon, Pennsylvania (the location of his Lodge) for a meeting in which he was recognized for his 50 years of service to our Masonic fraternity. The next day he boarded a bus and returned to Missouri.

This in itself is an extremely remarkable act, far beyond what I have experienced before, by a brother to receive this award. What is even more remarkable, about the effort, however, is that this brother traveled the distance with his seeing-eye dog as his only companion, for this brother is legally blind.

It must've been through efforts and interest of men like these that we have the privilege of being Freemasons today.

Brother Edwin Schickley is a remarkable man. He is also a remarkable Freemason.

I cannot help but wonder how much greater we might be if we had more Brothers as dedicated to the Craft as is this brother. He certainly has my admiration and respect. He deserves the same from all Freemasons.

On January 13th of this year, I received a report from brother Walter C. Heck of the Visitation Committee of one of our lodges. Along with the report was a letter in which this brother wrote: "Enclosed is a report of visitations for the year 1991. This is the 13th and final year of my visitations to the ill and shut-ins."

He went on to discuss the locations in three states, and in five counties in the Commonwealth of Pennsylvania to which he had journeyed in order to visit our brethren who were in the hospital. He closed his communication with, "I enjoyed doing visitations—why?—When I was ill with double pneumonia in January 1947 in the Norfolk Naval Hospital, the first person to visit me was a Mason of the Cape Charles, Virginia Masonic Lodge. I've never forgotten that."

I have been receiving these annual reports from Brother Heck for a number of years. His are the only ones which I have received.

We, as members of the Craft, can sit and lament the loss of the feeling of Brotherhood or we can, like Brother Heck, live Masonic Brotherhood. There is nothing I could add that would improve upon what he has done to maintain the image of our Craft.

[13]

The 275th Anniversary of the United Grand Lodge of England

On June 9, 10, and 11, I was afforded the opportunity and privilege to be with our R.W. Grand Master in attending the 275th anniversary of the United Grand Lodge of England. I will ever regard it as one of the greatest experiences of my life.

On Tuesday evening, June 9, we were greeted at a special reception in Guild Hall with a buffet dinner hosted by the Lord Mayor of London, a member of the Craft. Guild Hall is an old and impressive Gothic-style building and offered an environment which cannot be found in this country.

On Wednesday, Grand Lodge, presided over by his Royal Highness, the Most Worshipful Grand Master, the Duke of Kent, was opened in London's largest arena, Earl's Court, with 12,000 to 15,000 brethren present, the largest gathering in the history of Freemasonry. They represented eighty-four Grand Lodges, thirty-four, from the United States, also the largest combined representation of Grand Lodges.

It was inspiring to me to hear Most Worshipful Brother Joseph Ferencz, Grand Master of the Symbolic Grand Lodge of Hungary. Now elderly, he was Grand Master of the Grand Lodge of Hungary prior to World War II, when it was closed down by the Nazis and remained closed under Communism.

That evening, a banquet was held in which the toast was proposed by the representative of Most Worshipful Grand Master Prince Bertil of the Grand Lodge of Sweden, to which our Grand Master was honored to provide the response on behalf of the distinguished guests attending. His response was given with his usual capable aplomb, and he certainly represented our Grand Lodge extremely well.

During the day Thursday, there were discussion groups in Freemasons Hall and in the evening we were entertained by the Welsh Choir made up of Members of Lodges from Wales, presenting Brother Wolfgang Amadeus Mozart's *The Magic Flute*.

I know I will never live to see anything as impressive as was the processional into Grand Lodge with hundreds of our members and their distinctive Grand Lodge regalia from eighty-four jurisdictions. I only wish it were possible for every Freemason to have experienced the emotion that this gathering generated.

[14]

What Is Important

I recently finished reading a book titled *Priest and Freemason: The Life of George Oliver*. In reading it, I found myself thinking how sad it is that someone could have had as profound an effect upon the Masonic fraternity and be so little known by the membership today. I would be greatly surprised if even ten percent of our membership ever heard the name George Oliver, let alone know of his contribution.

For many years I have said, half jokingly, that a year after I'm dead people will ask, "Tom who?" I use this simple statement to help me to keep in perspective, lest I should ever forget, my relative importance in life—and yet—I find myself thinking back to friends I have known who have meant so much to Freemasonry being unknown so shortly after their death.

Reading this book, however, did cause me to recognize more fully that it is not the memory of the man nor the memory of his contribution, but the contribution itself that is important.

Each of us, in our own minds, acknowledges those in the past who have created a lasting impression upon us and helped mold us into what we are. We are in life, nothing more than a reflection of all of our life's experiences melded together by how they affected us. It is important, therefore, that each of us, as an individual, realizes that we, in turn,

31

can create a lasting influence upon what someone else will become.

Freemasonry is no different in this regard. It is today a resultant entity that has been created by those who formed it, developed it, and by those who influenced it. It is an obligation for us, therefore, to use all of our potential to create a positive image and influence upon those members of the Craft following us.

It would be well if each of us was familiar with the name George Oliver and the influence he created and his contribution to Freemasonry and, for that matter, all other great Masonic personalities. If we do not, however, recognize his name, and if we do not recognize his contribution, perhaps it is not all that important. But it is important that it was made. Without the contribution of George Oliver and many other men, Freemasonry would not be as we know it.

So even if we do not recognize, the Craft is, because the Craft does, and because the Craft does, the world does. This speculative Fraternity of ours has quietly created one of the greatest influences upon man, that the world has ever known. As it continues to evolve, our contributions to it and influences upon it will determine its destiny. We, the members, are its only internal variable. So although our names may be forgotten, our contributions may well be felt for many generations to come. We will leave a legacy to be passed through generations, so long as the Craft lives. Each of us has felt the effect of George Oliver's legacy, even if his name is unknown. His was positive. So, too, can be yours.

[15]

The Quality of the Man

Freemasonry has frequently been described as an organization whose purpose it is to take good men and make them better. This definition, out of necessity, therefore, implies selectivity—selectivity to the extent that we begin with good men.

Practically, however, we must realize that, human judgment being what it is, we will not always succeed in getting the good man. The second part of the definition, therefore, comes into play more importantly, making those new members into the best they can be.

I have been impressed many times in my Masonic journey by the improvement I have observed in men who have chosen to pass through the chairs of various Masonic Bodies. It is doubtful whether an exception can be made of any man being a better man when he completes the chairs than when he began. No man receiving the influence of Freemasonry can fail to be a better man.

It is a natural instinctive desire of most forms of life to associate with those of similar kind. This is why we find in nature, flocks, herds, schools, etc. of animals. This is no less true of "man." However, in man, we show a greater diversity of types and break into smaller groups based upon other variables. This most important variable in the case of Freemasonry is the quality of the man. We should expect, therefore, that there would be a tendency of good men wishing to associate with good men. Freemasonry has carried this concept long before and much further than any other organization.

Our Craft has been a unique organization in that it has been able to take men from all walks of life, socially, economically, culturally, etc., and provide an environment wherein the similarities of good are far more important than the differences of type.

I suspect the quality of the man is perhaps the major intangible force which, though unseen to the world outside of the Craft, is a major factor that has brought us together and keeps us together.

My friend, Brother Stuart M. L. Pollard, related the story that when Brother and Gen. Douglas MacArthur attended the first Lodge meeting in the Philippines following the liberation of Manila was recognized in the Lodge as the Supreme Allied Commander. His response to the Master of the Lodge was, "When I walked through the portals of this Lodge room, I dropped my cloak of authority as Supreme Allied Commander and assumed the title of Brother. I would appreciate being treated as such."

The experience of being able to sit with my Brothers and to be regarded by them as such, is the greatest privilege I can ever expect to receive other than being accepted by my God.

We must always remember that Freemasonry was never meant to be an organization for every man. There is nothing wrong in being selective. We became what we became because of selectivity. We are what we are because of selectivity. We will remain what we are only by retaining that selectivity. It is our obligation as Freemasons to keep the quality of the Craft the best that it can be by selecting only good men and making them better.

[16]

I Don't Have the Time

How many times in life have we heard someone say, "I don't have the time"? I read recently in the *Scottish Rite Journal* about a member who has not missed a Blue Lodge meeting in forty-six years and has been elected treasurer of his Lodge for thirty-five consecutive times. He is a Past Master and Life Member of his Lodge, Past High Priest and Life Member of his Chapter, Past Commander and Life Member of his Commandery, a member of the Knights of the York Cross of Honor, a Life Member, and holds the 33rd degree of the Ancient Accepted Scottish Rite.

He has sponsored more than one hundred petitions for each of the Masonic bodies in which he holds membership. In addition, he has donated to Brethren more than 100 permanent memberships in the Knights Templar Eye Foundation and more than 100 permanent contributing memberships in the Shrine Hospitals.

He is also a Past Potentate and Life Member of his Shrine Temple, a Life Member of the Grotto, a Life Member of the Scottish Rite Guard, an Emeritus Life Member of the Order of the Eastern Star, a Past Vice Chairman and Emeritus Member of the Board of Trustees of the Scottish Rite Children's Hospital, a Past President of his Masonic Temple Corporation, and a Past Master of his District Masonic Association.

He was President of his Masonic Temple Company for 10 years and was responsible to a great extent for the fiscal stability of the Lodges in that Temple. He was twice named President of the Scottish Rite Foundation of Georgia. This list merely touches upon his contributions to Freemasonry.

In looking at a man's Masonic career as extensive as this Brother's, one would assume that his life was totally devoted to Freemasonry. However, it is significant that along with many other civic activities, he was also Charter President of the Atlanta Law School Alumni Association, served as President of the Georgia Children's Chiropractic Center, Director of the Joseph B. Whitehead Memorial Boys Club, Chairman of the Board of Trustees of the Doctors Memorial Hospital for eight years and Vice Chairman for 10 years, and also, past president of the Overland Guaranty Insurance Agency. In 1930, at the age of 17, he became the youngest Deacon in the Presbytery of his church and in 1955, was elected to Elder.

Now, we can probably assume that his whole life was dedicated to service to organizations leaving time for little else. However, he earned his L.L.B. and L.L.M degrees from Atlanta Law School and an L.L.D. from Webster University. He worked for a period of time for the U.S. government and in 1954, became judge in the Criminal Court and is now judge Emeritus, Superior Court of Fulton County, Georgia.

The brother's name is Charles A. Wofford, actually Illustrious Brother, Judge Charles A. Wofford. To quote Brother Wofford, "Masonry expresses the highest ideals outside of the church of what I believe is a proper attitude of obedience to God and love for one's fellow man."

I guess the major difference between Brother Wofford and most of the rest of us is he did not say, "I don't have the time." Thank God for the Charles Woffords of the world.

[17]

Beyond the Ordinary

Some years ago, the then Sovereign Grand Commander of the Ancient and Accepted Scottish Rite, Southern Jurisdiction, Henry Clausen, wrote a book titled *Beyond the Ordinary*. Although Brother Clausen was not applying this title to Freemasonry, what a descriptive purpose it does imply!

Freemasonry's goal has always been to start with the best we can find and, through the teachings of our moral lessons, attempt to improve upon that best. None of us who have been active in Freemasonry can have failed to recognize the qualitative improvement in the members of our Craft as they continue to learn the meaning of these moral lessons.

It is not for every man to be great, but it is for every man to be greater than he will be. If Freemasonry can serve by being the motivation as well as the conduit which stimulates its members to become greater, what a purpose for being!

Unfortunately, man has a tendency to look up to those whom he regards as being superior to him, but at the same time to look down upon those whom he regards as not his equal. Such action diminishes the observer. Freemasonry teaches the equality of man, irrespective of position. We should always recognize that there is no one in life from whom we cannot learn something. We each become a reflection of all of our life's experiences modified by our personality. For that reason, we never know what a lasting influence another may have upon our life, nor do we know what a lasting influence we may have upon the life of another. Freemasonry, since its inception, has been an organization which has impacted positively the reflection of its members, and in this regard has always been "beyond the ordinary."

We have a tendency today to attempt to evaluate ourselves in terms of quantity instead of quality and, as a result, tend to lament that we may not be as great as we once were, simply because our numbers are not as high as they once were. This is an unfortunate appraisal of the Craft.

We must never forget the greatness of our history, but we must acknowledge that tomorrow is built upon today. Life is for today—not yesterday. We can become today what we want to become, but not by dreaming of the past. The following quotation I kept in the front of my classroom during my teaching years: "I had no shoes, and I cried, and then I met a man who had no feet." We do not rise by crying over what we lack. We must continue to improve what we have and build upon it. We must practice the basic precept that we are a Brotherhood of Man under the Fatherhood of God. After all, it is this precept above all others that has made Freemasonry, what it is.

Most of us will never leave any big mark on this world, but we can all leave some mark. We certainly can all be brothers and in so doing contribute immensely to the future of our Craft. A poet once wrote, "I sought my soul, but my soul I could not see. I sought my God, but my God eluded me. I sought my brother; I found all three." Think about it—so simple a thought yet so "beyond the ordinary."

[18]

A Brotherhood Undivided

The dedication of the Friend to Friend—A Brotherhood Undivided Monument now rests in the annals of history of the Grand Lodge of Pennsylvania. The impact of that dedication, however, will remain fixed in the memories and in the hearts of those who had the privilege to experience it.

The sculptor, Brother Ron Tunison, has captured in bronze and frozen in time, the very soul of the Craft expressing the truest meaning of Brotherhood.

For years, the members of the Jurisdiction of Pennsylvania have learned of the significance of the heritage of Pennsylvania Freemasonry with the existence of the Masonic Temple in Philadelphia and the Masonic Homes in Elizabethtown. Now the Memorial in Gettysburg must rank as a third. The significance of this monument will create a mecca for Masonic pilgrimages for generations to come.

I will always remember seeing visiting Grand Masters with tears on their cheeks, tears created by the impact of their first view of the sculpture when it was unveiled. I will remember the poignancy of the occasion when the descendents of General Armistead and Captain Bingham, who never met before this occasion, stood together at night before this lighted monument. I will remember the thrill of pride enveloping me—because I was a Freemason. I will remember the feeling of Brotherhood exuding from friends I had known, and friends I had not known, but friends because we were Brothers.

Most Worshipful Brother George P. Pulkkinen, Grand Master of the Grand Lodge of Maine wrote following the dedication: "For years, perhaps forever, Freemasons have attempted to share the message of Freemasonry with those around us. I daresay that never has that concept been shared so eloquently as you have done with the Friend to Friend Masonic Memorial. The powerful message of Brother helping Brother, under the direst of circumstances, speaks most powerfully of man's ability and willingness—to go out of our way to serve a fallen Brother, it is truly ennobling."

In all ages, great accomplishments have begun with great dreams. This monument will stand to remind us that the dreams of a few can become the reality of many. Freemasonry still dreams the impossible dream and with unanimity of purpose creates the reality.

We, as Pennsylvania, Freemasons, must never for a moment forget our heritage. We must also, however, never forget the obligation to preserve that heritage. I encourage each of you to make a special effort not only to visit the monument in Gettysburg, but also the other major Masonic structures within Pennsylvania which have become our heritage and of which we are the caretakers.

Brother Pulkkinen concluded, "I thank the Brethren of Pennsylvania for having the wisdom, the courage, the commitment, and the dedication to share this powerful truth with the men, women and children of the United States and beyond."

So mote it ever be.

[19]

John J. Robinson, a Man and a Mason

I n the last issue of *The Pennsylvania Freemason*, we noted the death of Brother John J. Robinson, Master Mason. His contribution to the Craft, however, is of such magnitude that it would be a gross oversight to do no more than note his passing. Brother John was a truly remarkable individual, yet there was so little known about him.

He first appeared upon the Masonic scene with the publication of the book, *Born in Blood*. It is doubtful whether any publication concerning Freemasonry (other than possibly the first exposés) ever created a greater impact than did this volume. It is significant that John Robinson was not a professional writer and that it was the first writing he attempted. He did so, following retirement from a field of management and financial consulting. He also was a co-inventor of a method for producing plastic eyeglass lenses.

Many individuals, upon retirement, seek to find ways to avoid ongoing mental challenges. Not so, Brother Robinson. He continued in his new-found endeavor by writing a second book, *Dungeon, Fire and Sword*, a medieval history dealing with the Knights Templar and the Crusades. Finally, his third and last book, *A Pilgrim's Path: One Man's Road to the Masonic Temple*, was published shortly before his death. All three volumes were written before John affiliated with the Masonic Fraternity. Few professional writers ever achieve the success that he did.

I have met few men in my life, with whom I developed as close a friendship in such a short period of time as I did with John. It was my great privilege to be asked by him to be one of his recommenders for membership in Freemasonry (granted by the Grand Lodge of Ohio) and to be the speaker at a banquet in the Valley of Cincinnati when, John became a Scottish Rite Mason.

A notation in the last *Pennsylvania Freemason* indicated that he contributed more in a short period of time to the Fraternity than most do in a lifetime. (When John died, he had been a member of the Craft for less than one year.) I was also afforded the sad opportunity to express my feelings at John's memorial service and during this service, was a little more emphatic. I stated that the influence John created upon Freemasonry in three years, was greater than what all of us sitting in that room would create in the combined years of our lives.

It is doubtful whether any of us will live long enough to experience again a personality who will impact the Craft and for some of us, impact our lives as much as did John Robinson. His ability to work and to see, to analyze and to define Freemasonry and Freemasons required not only the interest, but also the analytical mind that provides the insight to do so. John's capability not only to make the analysis, but also to express it in his inimitable way, displayed a uniqueness found in few men. He advanced from being a Masonic unknown to being a Masonic giant in a span of just three years.

John Robinson served as an example, unparalleled by what an intelligent man studying extensively the subject of Freemasonry can deduce for justification in becoming a member of the Craft. No man has ever become a Freemason better equipped to understand why. He traveled over

150,000 miles in his last two years, not only eloquently defending Freemasonry against those who have chosen to become its enemies, but also in promoting Freemasonry because of its principles which he so greatly admired.

Freemasonry has lost one of its greatest members and greatest friends, and I sadly acknowledge that loss. Only three years did I know him, yet in those three years he became a colleague, a confidant and a friend. As I stated in Cincinnati, however, I do not express regret that John died—I thank God that John lived.

[20]

Do We Give too Much
and Require too Little?

Freemasonry has been linked historically with a concern for youth for many years. We have developed and supported our youth organizations — the Order of DeMolay, the Order of Rainbow for Girls and the Order of Job's Daughters. Even before their creation, however, probably back to the inception of the Craft, we have expressed a concern for young people. In studying the history of Freemasonry, we note that one of the great concerns has always been the care of widows and orphans. The concern has been expressed in our operation of homes and schools for the orphaned and for the socially disadvantaged youth. We have become more supportive of their goals of higher education in our recent years.

I quote part of a letter I received from a young lady who received one of our Higher Education Loans.

Dear Mr. Jackson,

As of December 15, 1991, we graduated from Bloomsburg University of Pennsylvania with a bachelors degree.... I say "we" because without the support and generosity of you and your fellow Brothers, I may not have received the finances to continue my education. I would like to thank you on behalf of all the students you have supported and the students who will seek your help in the future. Sometimes we forget to thank those who deserve it the most.

I have received many similar letters in the past, and they are heartening, to say the least, since I also receive many letters and telephone calls criticizing our program because we require repayment of the loans even though a loan note is required.

At the direction of our R.W. Grand Master, I wrote a brief paper on youth development, to be presented to the Executive Committee of the Grand Lodge. In it, I expressed a concern that perhaps we require too little from the youth of today. A considerable portion of my life was dedicated to working with young people as a professional in the teaching field and as a volunteer leader in the Boy Scouts of America and the Order of DeMolay. During those years, I observed the distressing decline in initiative to excel. I firmly believe that this decline is at least in part due to what we as adults required or rather did not require.

Most of the leaders of Freemasonry today acknowledge the lack of interest of at least two generations of young people reflected by the decline in membership in those age brackets. We fail, however, at times to consider deeply enough the cause of the lack of interest.

I noted in my last years in the teaching profession the continuing loss of interest in others by young people. Self-centeredness became a way of life in our society, and it has only been in recent years that I've been able to detect a redevelopment of that interest. Any organization dedicated to helping others would suffer in this type of climate.

I would suggest that much of a problem today has been a result of our continuing attitude that each generation continue to make life easier for each succeeding generation. In the process, we have unfortunately forgotten the necessity of teaching responsibility. The result has been many young people today have developed an attitude that what they receive is owed to them. Defaults in the guaranteed loan program of the federal government are unfortunately, classic, and now, amount to hundreds of millions of dollars which the taxpayers must pick up.

Most evidence indicates that the general trend of thought regarding the direction of the youth of our country as has been practiced in recent years has been incorrect. Our continuing to give, requiring little in return has not only not benefited our youth, but has also proven detrimental. As long as we as a nation have the attitude that we can buy the admiration and respect of our youth by giving more while requiring less, we have little or no hope of recapturing that admiration or respect.

This is the reason I feel so pleased when I receive a letter such as the one quoted in this article. It shows me that, in what may have become a general attitude, there continues to exist the islands of hope. I am thoroughly convinced that one of the great contributions Freemasonry can make is to teach the young people with whom we come in contact, responsibility. We must seek for, and strive to develop the highest quality of performance in the youth of the world. It is no less true in teaching the young than it is in dealing with the adult—that the less we require the less we receive. If we direct our youth toward a concept of quality, we give them a reason for pride and accomplishment. We must continue to provide the help, but we must also emphasize the need to instill responsibility. Therein we build the leaders of tomorrow.

[21]

The Flowing Stream of Freemasonry

I recall a quotation I heard many years ago, "when you place your hand in a flowing stream, you touch the last that has gone before and the first that is yet to come."

A man's relevant position in history and our position in Freemasonry is as that hand. We stand today as the hand in the flowing stream of Freemasonry touching the last that has gone before and the first that is yet to come. There is a distinctive difference, however, between the hand in the water and us. The hand has no power to change the ultimate destiny of the flow of the water. But we, my brethren, have the capacity and the power to change the ultimate destiny of Freemasonry. Indeed, what we are doing today will determine where Freemasonry is in all of the tomorrows.

Regretfully, many members of our Craft will not only leave no Fraternal impact, but will not even leave evidence of their presence. Yet, we all have the capability of doing so. If each of us influenced only one man in a way that caused him to see the greatness of our Fraternity, that influence could change his life and thus be passed on to generations yet unborn.

Our R. W. Grand Master has instituted a new program in Pennsylvania Freemasonry, known as Friend to Friend. Since influential effect is self-perpetuating, this program offers to each of us the opportunity to extend our influence through the ages. It is designed not only to influence, but also to have a major impact on our Fraternity's future. It is to function as an educational program to let those outside the Craft know who we are what we do. It is a program, not just to increase the quantity of the Craft, but to improve quality through the education of quality men. The quality man is out there. Our goal must be to educate him as to the value of Freemasonry to him, to society and to the world.

I am convinced that Freemasonry's greatness is a result of two major precepts which guide our practices: (1) We have provided an environment whereby men of all walks of life could sit as equals and (2) we have attracted the greatest minds available in all ages. Our future depends on retaining these precepts.

When we evolved from a Fraternity of the practitioner to a Fraternity of the idealist, we forged the character of an organization that was idealistic. We must never lose that idealism. Society needs that character, perhaps more than ever before. Freemasonry was the source from which it was drawn in the past; it can be now, and it can remain so in the future.

The Friend of Friend program has provided each one of us with the opportunity to ensure not only a Masonic future, but a GREAT Masonic future. It is our fervent hope that each of you will be a part of that future. May it never be said of us that we failed to direct the flowing stream of Freemasonry to anything but a glowing future of contribution to mankind. Thus, we will be as we have always been.

[22]

If We Each Influenced Only One Man

Following the last *Pennsylvania Freemason* issue, I received a communication from my good friend, Brother Stuart M. L. Pollard, former Executive Secretary of the Masonic Service Association. In it he stated, "really think you should expand on the second paragraph."

The second paragraph read: "Regretfully, many members of our Craft will not only leave no fraternal impact, but will not even leave evidence of their presence. Yet, we all have the capability of doing so. If we each influenced only one man in a way that caused him to see the greatness of our Fraternity, that influence could change his life, and thus be passed on through generations yet unborn."

I gave thought to Brother Pollard's suggestion and am devoting this column to an expansion on that paragraph. The impact of this thought is monumental in its effect, if applied. Monumental, not only in the influence on the man, but also on the Craft.

The Grand Lodge of Pennsylvania currently has approximately 160,000 members. If each influenced just one man in a way that caused them see the greatness of the Craft and become a Freemason, our membership would be 320,000 by this time next year. And, if each of these influenced just one man, our membership would be 480,000. Expand that concept to the approximately 2.3 million members in the United States. We would increase our membership to 4.6 million and then to 6.9 million and onward. The resulting force upon this many good men would have to impact our continuously evolving society.

I realize that the practicality of this concept stretches into the realm of the improbable, and yet each one of us has been influenced by someone to become what we are. I also realize that Freemasonry means different things to different members and that it is not as important in the lives of some as it is in the lives of others. It must be assumed, however, that it has to be important in some way for a member simply to pay his dues annually to retain his membership. If there is a value of that membership to him, it must be of value to other qualified friends of his.

My Brothers, Freemasonry, has done so much to influence our lives, and even if it has been less on a personal basis for some of the members then it has for others, its impact on the development of modern civil society on a worldwide basis provide stimulus enough to let the world know our philosophy, our principles and our practices. Each of us is a living example of the Craft. Who we are and what we do is what those not part of us see and respond to. I recall reading of an old man being honored for having been a Mason for 70 years. When called upon, he said he set his sights to become a Mason, when, as a small boy, he observed within the community a group of men with outstanding character and reputation, and he learned they were Freemasons. I wonder how many small boys are looking at us and setting their sights to become Freemasons, because of what we represent to them.

We cannot afford to lessen our potential to contribute to civilization, our lessons which perhaps laid the foundations for the concept of social equality. Freemasonry emphasizes the importance of toleration, probably to a greater degree than any organization conceived by man.

The practice of toleration could today go a long, long way in solving the major problems of the world.

In the last issue, I wrote of the value of the Friend to Friend program in providing a mechanism through which we can distribute to those outside of our Craft knowledge of who we are and what we do. In looking back on my life, I must acknowledge that anything I have achieved. I did so with the help of others, although I did not realize it at the time. Now the time has come to repay. I trust that my life has served to influence others to become part of us. I would hope that all of us feel the same way. Whatever Fraternal impact we may leave upon the Craft could very well continue to impact the ongoing evolution of civil society. All we need do is influence one man or serve as an example for a small boy.

[23]

Friend to Friend

I assume that those who read this column have read a
number of my writings. Many of you have also heard
me speak. In all probability, some of you have not always
agreed with my thoughts and opinions. However, I don't
think anyone can disagree with my devotion and dedication
to this Craft. Over half my life has been one of concern
with keeping Freemasonry a viable force in the world.

One of the first Masonic speeches I developed almost thirty years ago was devoted to my concern about
membership decline, and some will remember that I have
concentrated much of my efforts to writing and speaking
on this concern. Today I speak and write frequently on the
quality as well as the quantity of the Craft. It is necessary,
my Brothers, to have quality of membership, but we need
the quantity to support the magnitude of our efforts. If
we take the time to recognize what Freemasonry has accomplished, we also must recognize the need to maintain
a membership to continue to accomplish.

We have for years now, tried to stem the quality and
quantity decline without success. We live in an age where
helping one another is not as important as it once was, so
our need is not as visible as it once was. We have been experiencing, on a Grand Lodge level, for more than fifteen
years, the frustration of trying to solve a dilemma that
seems insolvable, but now the answer is here. The Friend

to Friend program, if used in the manner it was intended to be used, may solve the problems of both quantity and quality.

Some of our members have not given full support to Friend to Friend because they think it is a solicitation program. IT IS NOT. It is designed to be an educational program—a program wherein we have the opportunity to let the good qualified man know who we are and what we do. I doubt whether anyone could oppose solicitation anymore than I do. Freemasonry has always operated under the philosophy that if we are great enough others will seek us, but we must let those qualified men know that we are here. I am convinced that Friend to Friend is the best program, that could be devised to give each of us an opportunity to let those men who would make good members know we are here. It does not lessen the responsibility of any of us to make sure that the man we recommend is Masonic quality material.

One has to wonder how many good men who might have been good Masons, or even great men who might've been great Masons, never became so because they did not even know we existed or, if they knew we existed, did not know who we were what we did. A recent national survey revealed that 45% of all men over the age of 21 never heard of Freemasonry, and less than 10% knew how to join.

I became a Freemason, when a friend of mine said to me, "Tom, you should be a Freemason." This was not an invitation to join, it was a statement of his evaluation of me. Yet to this day, there are those within the Craft who sincerely believe they cannot talk about it.

How sad, and what a loss to Freemasonry and to the world! Freemasonry's future is in the hands of each of us today. It is imperative that we are united in our effort to increase the quantity of good men in the Craft. The Friend of Friend program gives us the tools. We may not get an-other chance. If we truly believe in the philosophy of the Brotherhood of Man and the Fatherhood of God, if we truly believe that this philosophy can make a difference, then we welcome you to become part of a program that will impact our future.

[24]

The Boy Scouts of America:
A Rich Proving Ground
for Masonic Members

S everal weeks ago, someone suggested to me that, since 1995, is the 85th anniversary of the Boy Scouts of America and since I was active in scouting for many years and because of the similarity in philosophy with Freemasonry, I might wish to write on that subject sometime.

An article recently appeared in the *Wall Street Journal* discussing the "graying" of the Shrine. Specifically, the article dealt with the aging of the members of the Shrine with the concomitant loss of membership, which must accompany an organization with aging membership. It is well documented that as the average age of the Shriner increases the average age of the Mason also increases.

In this article, it was noted that the Shrine was looking to stimulate an interest in membership through fraternities on college campuses. This approach sounds logical, inasmuch as college fraternities stimulate a feeling of brotherhood and, camaraderie which, if perpetuated into adulthood, should lead to an interest in organizations like Freemasonry.

Our greatest increases in membership have historically followed periods of war. This increase has likewise been the result of the feeling of brotherhood and camaraderie which men developed during wartime experience. There can be little doubt that this feeling is a large motivating factor in men uniting together to organizational membership.

I was very active in the Boy Scouts for more than twenty years and state unequivocally that I have achieved whatever success I have because of the initial impact of scouting in my life. I did not have the opportunity to be a member of the Order of DeMolay, which I sincerely regret, but I was a Boy Scout, and must credit the Boy Scouts of America for being a guiding force in my life.

I've been pleasantly surprised over the years at the number Freemasons who stop me when I am wearing my National Eagle Scout Association lapel pin and tell me that they also are Eagle Scouts. Yet, why should I be surprised?

The basic principles of the Boy Scouts of America, as those in DeMolay, are not at all unlike the basic principles of Freemasonry. They require belief in God, and have staunchly defended that requirement in recent years. They require by the Scout Oath that members do their best to do their duty to God and Country. The twelve points of the Scout Law are indicative of all the qualities we expect to find as members of the Masonic fraternity. There is in fact an organization of Freemasons, who are also Eagle Scouts. So again I ask, why should I be surprised?

It was the Boy Scouts that taught me the importance of an inter-relationship with other people and how to be a leader. It was the Boy Scouts that taught me that it was easier to be a friend than a foe. It was a Boy Scouts that taught me not to learn hate and fear. It was the Boy Scouts that taught me the first basic qualities which I found in Freemasonry, and probably most important of all, it was a Boy Scouts who first taught me the meaning of the brotherhood of man.

I was talking with General Westmoreland last year when we were speaking together at the Vietnam Memorial, and I commented that it was always good to meet another

Eagle Scout. He came back later to me to ask what vintage and I told him 1951. He laughed and said, "mine is 1929." It was then, more than in the past, that I recognized the unbreakable bond of the Boy Scout organization. It is that same bond which characterizes Freemasonry. It is that bond which I have had the great privilege to experience in so many ways and so many different locations in the world.

When I began contemplating what to write about in this column following the reading of the article in The Wall Street Journal, I began to think that perhaps the Boy Scouts of America might be a great place to look for future members of Freemasonry. We look today to the Order of DeMolay as a normal transition into Masonic membership. Why not look to the Boy Scouts of America for the same?

There is a great similarity between their teachings and the teachings of the Order of DeMolay. The only major difference I can observe is the lack of ritual found in DeMolay. The greatest preparation for man would probably have been to have the opportunity to experience membership in both of these organizations. They indeed could almost be regarded as a proving ground of the quality youth and the training ground for the quality man.

We all know that if the philosophy of Freemasonry were practiced worldwide, many of man's greatest problems would be solved. We teach a form of Brotherhood found in few organizations requiring a belief in a Supreme Being. This brotherhood is found in both youth organizations— DeMolay and Boy Scouts.

Freemasonry has proven its importance to the world and so too, has the Boy Scouts of America. I am proud to have been accepted by both. I suggest a natural progression could be from Boy Scout to Freemason. It is the largest youth organization in the world. Perhaps we should consider the prospect.

[25]

Freemasonry in Pennsylvania
and Around the World

In September, I received a telephone call from a friend in Paris, who is also the Assistant Grand Master of the National Grand Lodge of France. He asked authorization to purchase and to use our Friend to Friend brochure by the English speaking lodges operating under the National Grand Lodge of France.

This request is an indication of the ongoing impact that our Friend to Friend program is creating on Freemasonry. Approximately twenty grand lodges, both in this country and outside of it, are using the program as an educational tool to inform non-members of the significance of our Craft. We receive ongoing inquiries from Grand Lodges in North America as to how to use the Friend to Friend program.

We also received numerous calls and letters thanking us for Friend to Friend. I quote one:

Dear Worshipful Brother Jackson,
It is with great joy and gratitude to the Grand Lodge of Pennsylvania for promptly sending to us, the eloquent Friend to Friend brochures that we asked for. We have never experienced such genuine unanimity of enthusiasm. You are to be congratulated for sharing this wonderful vehicle presenting our beloved Masonic

Fraternity to our friends so tactfully. We have great faith that this brochure will promote great universal growth to our Masonic Fraternity. "Blessed be the tie that binds us in Masonry."

The Grand Lodge of Canada in the Province of Ontario adopted the brochure and changed the front cover, so that those famous Freemasons displayed were Canadians. The Grand Lodge of India contacted me in August to let me know that they are planning to do the same thing, using famous Freemasons of India for the cover. We have received communications from several other Grand Lodges outside of North America asking to use the program or to discuss its merits, including the Grand Lodge of Western Australia and the Grand Lodge of Greece. I have been informed, although I have no documentation, that the Grand Lodge of Israel is also making use of the program in some form.

In my sixteen years as Grand Secretary, I have never experienced this type of reaction by other Grand Jurisdictions. It is indicative of the great concern the Masonic leaders have today for the future of the Craft. I have expressed many times, my feelings that the future of Freemasonry lies within our abilities and dedication to educate both the member and the non-member of the character of Freemasonry. Several issues ago I raised the question, "How many good men who might have become great Masons never became so, simply because they never heard of us?" Used properly, this program can fill that void. The man must still ask, and the member must still vouch for the quality of the man. Friend to Friend does not change that.

With the use of Friend to Friend, the Grand Lodge of Wyoming had an increase in membership for the first time in thirty-three years. Our Grand Lodge continues to show the benefit of utilization of the program, but we have yet to approach any numbers resulting in a net increase in membership. I have been wondering why Wyoming's results have differed so from ours, and there probably is no single answer to that question. The Grand Lodge of Wyoming has far fewer members than does the Grand Lodge of Pennsylvania, and on a numerical basis alone, it would be easier to show an increase. But percentage-wise, it would be an erroneous assumption to think that this is the sole answer since a population of the entire state of Wyoming is less than half a million.

I have been visiting in Wyoming for a number of years and have found that a relationship existing between Brothers is far more personable than we tend to find in our jurisdiction. This factor probably has a great deal to do with the degree of success, which has resulted in that jurisdiction. This Craft characteristic also seems to exist more strongly in most jurisdictions outside of the United States. The Brotherly bond between members has been one of the strongest factors which led to success, even if for a limited time in all fraternities. The very name Fraternal means brotherly. Freemasonry has coupled this Brotherhood of Man with the Fatherhood of God, and the result has been the greatest Fraternity of all time.

Perhaps we've tended to forget too much the Brother in the Brotherhood of Man under the Fatherhood of God. This can easily happen in this fast-paced world we live in today. If this is what is happening, then more than the Craft is the loser. Make no doubt about it, my Brothers, this world needs us, and it needs our philosophy. We must let the world know. We cannot exclude Brother from Brotherhood and remain Freemasonry.

If the more Brotherly personable relationship of the past, sustained our greatness, and I believe it was an important factor, then it was probably a significant part of

Wyoming's success. We must always be willing to study and to learn from both the success and the failure of others. Only by learning ourselves can we hope to educate others, and education is our hope for the future.

[26]

Freemasonry's Universal Constancy in Writings of Authors Worldwide

I have found myself in recent years reading books, parts of which all of our members should read. They reveal the constancy of universal thought and meaning of Freemasonry by many authors. Written by both members and nonmembers, they do credit to the Craft. I use this space to quote from some of those books. I only ask that when you read them you give them some thought. Many put my thoughts into words in a way I wish I could. The ones I use have been written by members of lodges in, Africa, England, and the Philippines and some by a female author.

> "Even if my thoughts and ideas may be controversial or, in certain respects, opened to question, I shall have succeeded in my attempt, if these ideas have generated further thoughts on the main substance of Freemasonry, in the search for universal truth and the unity of God."

> "It is only Masonic Education that will assure us that the brethren shall be more knowledgeable, conscious and concerned with the canons of Freemasonry. To do otherwise is to fail in our mission to filter and purify the brethren with the romance and beauty of Freemasonry."

"Freemasonry is not a secret society, but, even if it were, the tenants and principles practiced by the Order are so elevating that no one need be ashamed of them. In Freemasonry, the design of the Great Architect of the Universe is imprinted on all the principles of truth, love, and benevolence which are not confined to any single creed, race, group, people, or organization. In Freemasonry, the brethren can and should dwell together in brotherly concord."

"Masonry has proved to be too strong for jealousy, hate, fears and wars. Freemasonry has succeeded in bringing man nearer to man, and man nearer to God."

"Don't expect perfection in a man just because he is a Freemason. If you do, you will be disappointed. The aim and purpose of Freemasonry is to receive none but good men, keep them good and make them better. Judge the institution, not by a few failures, but by the average of its successes."

"Masonry is worth to us all that we are worth to it—neither more or less. Many complain that there's nothing in Masonry, forgetting that they have put nothing into it."

"The Craft can do much in the transformation of character, but it cannot transform material. Hence, you will appreciate that the Craft will give a brother what he has not, but it cannot make him what he is not."

"Some Masons regrettably find deep satisfaction in being associated with the Craft, simply to attach the feelings of respect, dignity and fear to their empty egos."

"Accommodations to personal request should not color our decisions and make us deviate from the duty with which we were charged. We should tilt the balance of admission in favor of the quality of a few than the quantity of the undeserving. For the health and betterment of the Craft, rigorous and stringent admission of candidates is eminently supreme."

"Freemasonry was one of the social practices that put freedom and equality central on the word list."

"If we shall not be careful in the admission of candidates and improve on the procedure of admission we are then starting the composition of a funeral hymn for the death of our noble institution. As Freemasons, we should not allow this to happen. If and when we do, we are doomed for we have just hammered the last nail and the sarcophagus of Freemasonry."

"Freemasonry assisted in the propagation of a mesmerist materialism and thus helped lay the foundation of democratic thought."

"And when the Great Architect of the Universe shall call my number and I shall stand naked and alone, before the Great White Throne and HE shall ask about my nation and my organization, with my head held high, looking straight into HIS eyes, I would with humility be proud to respond, FILIPINO, Sir, and a FREEMASON."

[27]

Freemasonry Is Primary

In recent years I have become more of a student of Free-masonry than I was in the past, and although I hesitate to think of myself as a Masonic scholar, there are those who tend to put me into that category. Whether I've become a student or scholar of the Craft is not as significant as is my recognition of the great dearth of Masonic students and scholars in present-day Freemasonry, as compared with the past. I doubt whether any would deny that one of the greatest problems facing Freemasonry today is a lack of knowledge of what it truly is, and this includes both a Mason, as well as the non-Mason. We simply have far too great a percentage of our membership unwilling to make the effort to understand the true philosophy and meaning of our fraternity.

The story is told of an old French doctor who devoted his life to his patients giving much of himself and requiring little in return. If they could not afford to pay, he made no charge. When the day approached that the old doctor could no longer continue in his profession, his patients wanted to give something to the old man in return for the devotion and unselfish contributions he made to their lives. However, they were too poor to give the old doctor, the type of recognition, which they felt he deserved. Each, however, produced wine for his own use. They decided that each would make a contribution of one pitcher of wine and they would present the doctor with a barrel of wine from which he could draw as he relaxed following retirement.

When the inevitable day came and the speeches of recognition and gratitude were completed, the old doctor, accepted the wine from those he served so long and so well, and he returned to his home. He drew a glass from the barrel of wine and sat down in a chair to relax. When he tasted the wine, however, it tasted like water. Thinking that something must be wrong, he took a second glass, but it also tasted like water, and sadly, the truth was revealed.

Each one of his patients felt that he had too little for his own use, and that he could not afford to contribute to the doctor. Each reasoned that since so many others were giving, his small contribution would not be missed.

How sad, and yet how true, that this analogy can also be applied to our Fraternity today. So many feel that their little contribution will not be missed, and as a result Freemasonry, like the old doctor, who meant so much to so many, experiences, the disappointment.

The more familiar I become with this organization, the more impressed I become with the magnitude of the impact that it is made in the world as we know it today. There can be no doubt that without Freemasonry, the civilized world, in its present form, probably would not exist. But, we are tending to become a passive Fraternity as non-involvement becomes more of a part of our lives. Each of us probably takes great pride in being able to point to so many great men that have been part of Freemasonry. Yet this tendency to point to the great man has led us to ignore the greatness of the Craft. It is the greatness of the organization with its philosophies and precepts which attracted the great men to begin with, and which made the world what it is today. Freemasonry is primary; membership is secondary. Without the greatness of the Craft, its composition would have been irrelevant. Yet at the same time, it was the contribution of the membership, which made the philosophy of the Craft work.

We should never cease to be proud of our past; but we can ill-afford to dwell upon it, if it causes us to lose sight of the present. Every single contribution, regardless of how small, is a contribution to the perpetuation of an ideal—perhaps the greatest ideal—that the mind of man has ever conceived. In an age that continues to see the world's major conflicts taking place in the name of God and religion, the philosophy of toleration is still as desperately needed as it was in the past. We find no organization today espousing a similar philosophy. We can continue to express our lovely platitudes and make no contribution; or we can be what we say we are, and practice what we preach.

There can be little doubt, however, that if we continue to fail to know what we are, we will continue to fail to be what we were. Probably the greatest challenge facing Masonic leadership today is the education of the membership of the true meaning of Freemasonry. Pennsylvania has been extremely fortunate in the field of Masonic education. We have had and continue to have, one of the greatest Masonic education programs in operation of any Grand Lodge in the world. But, as has been said many times, you cannot run 20,000 volts through a non-conductor and, unfortunately, too many of our members today have become non-conductors by choice. If we do not understand the Craft, how can we ever hope for the those outside to understand us.

If we continue to think that our little contribution will not be missed, then like the old doctor, an organization which has greatly impacted this world for close to 300 years during the evolution of civilization is like him—doomed to be disappointed. Think about it, my brothers, your contribution, no matter how small, is significant.

It's the Mason as Man
Who Has Impacted History

For a considerable number of years I have been wondering how an organization with as much influence as Freemasonry has had over several hundred years, could fail to be acknowledged for its contribution to the development of modern civilization and human thought. I even developed a talk which I titled "How can they ignore us?" In it, I asked those to whom I am speaking, how often they ever saw Freemasonry presented in a history text. I simply was unable to comprehend how we could be ignored.

With the exception of organized religion, Freemasonry probably has had a greater beneficial impact upon the development of present-day civilization than any other organization which has existed on earth, and yet, when you read historical documentation of the evolution of civilization Freemasonry is rarely mentioned and, if it is, it is only peripherally.

Last year the first World Conference of Grand Masters was held in Mexico City. Out of that conference came the Charter of Anahuac. The third item in the charter presented the need of the Craft in the twenty-first century to "to fight against…ecological depredation, contamination of the environment…, social instability…and religious commitments in education," amongst others.

I have a very serious concern with any proposal that

suggests Freemasonry's involvement in political and/or religious issues, and item three in the charter suggests precisely that. There is no way social and ecological issues can be dealt with, without involving politics or religion. This Craft has been able to weather the storms which wiped out many organizations and even toppled governments because it stayed above the controversies of religion and politics.

When I presented my concerns about the charter to some Masonic leaders, the rebuttal I received was that Masonry must have been involved in political and religious issues in the past. Freemasonry's influence in the American Revolution was cited as an example. They pointed to the actions of men like Washington, Franklin, Lafayette and others as Masonic involvement. In addition, Simon Bolivar in South America, Giuseppe Garibaldi in Italy, Lajos Kosuth in Hungary, Theodore Kolokotronis in Greece, Benito Juarez in Mexico, amongst many others who contributed so much to the concept of freedom, were examples of political involvement in other countries.

And then, for the first time, I began to understand why the influence of Freemasonry was not discussed in history books. We cannot deny the impact of Washington and many others in the development of American freedom, but it was Washington, the man, not Washington, the Mason, and not Freemasonry that made America what it is. This is also true of Bolivar, Kosuth, Kolokotronis and Juarez and all the other great patriots of their countries.

The philosophical purpose of Freemasonry is to develop the man—to start with good men and make them better, to increase the intellectual capacity of the individual, and to give the man, the incentive through our lessons to contribute to making the world a better place to live.

As an ecologist, I have for more than thirty-five years expressed my views on ecological issues and on the population explosion; but I speak as a man, not as a Freemason. My compassionate thought of life might have been nurtured in a Masonic Lodge, but, when I speak, it is not Freemasonry speaking. When Washington acted, it was not Freemasonry acting. Thankfully, Freemasonry has had a great influence on many leaders, but the man influenced does the acting. Thus we read about the man in history texts, not the organization.

So, now I understand why Freemasonry does not occupy a prominent place in history books, but that does not lessen its place in history. It probably would behoove historians to discuss the influence of Freemasonry on the man, and perhaps that is starting to occur.

[29]

Why You Joined Freemasonry

No one joins any organization without some reason for doing so, be it a church, social club, civic organization, union, or any other. A reason was there. Have you ever given time to think about why you joined Freemasonry?

In some cases, it might've been a passive reason, i.e., affiliation with the same religion or church in which you were raised. In others, an active stimulus might have been the factor, as in a political affiliation, but the cause was there. Now, my brothers, why did you become a member of our Craft?

Some years ago, an old man was being honored for having been a Freemason for 70 years. When asked to respond that night, he said that when he was a boy growing up in a small village, he observed a group of men in the community who were leaders with outstanding reputation and character. He learned that these men were Freemasons, and because of them. He reasoned that Masonry must be good, and set his sights on becoming a Freemason.

I just finished reading a new book, *Revolutionary Brotherhood* by Steven C. Bullock, which emphasized reasons for joining Freemasonry during more than 100 years of American history. I was somewhat amazed to learn the changes Freemasonry went through during those years, not only in its structural composition and operation, but also in its emphasis on different aspects of its operation. I knew that the Craft was not static; but I did not know enough of its evolution, which, in turn, produced different stimuli for affiliation.

One constant denominator that did not vary, however, through all its evolution was the emphasis on the quality of its membership, which in turn, probably has been the primary reason for most affiliations.

Today we are greatly concerned with the decline in our membership. Yet, by the simple practice of Freemasonry, we would aid in the reduction of declining membership.

If we became a Freemason with no mercenary or other improper motive, as we said we did; and, if we truly have made an effort to understand our obligation, then we would know that we owe to the past, and comprehend our obligation to the future.

Our late brother Johann Wolfgang von Goethe, the great German author and philosopher, many years ago wrote, "That which has been bequeathed to us must be earned anew if we would possess it." It would be well to remember that. I wonder how many small boys are watching us and reasoning that Masonry must be good and by that observation and reasoning are setting their sights on becoming Freemasons.

[30]

A Sleeping Giant?

I have heard Masonic leaders in recent years, refer to Freemasonry, as a sleeping giant, and in one of my talks, which I prepared a dozen years ago I also referred to it as a sleeping giant. Now I pause to think and to wonder why. I wonder not only about why a giant, but also I wonder why sleeping. The sleeping aspect is readily comprehensible when we consider the relative quiescence of Freemasonry today as compared to our past. But why is it not awake? The implication of being a giant begs definition. If Freemasonry may be accurately defined as a "giant," what qualities does it possess, which places it in that position?

In the year 1717, when speculative Freemasonry had its formal beginning and during the preceding years when it existed informally, it was a period in history when ethical and moral values were at low ebb and the influence of religion was being challenged. That time was probably ripe for the birth of an organization which promoted what we regard as admirable ethical and moral principles and a stimulus to an intellectual pursuit. In retrospect, we could probably say the time was ripe for the birth of a perspective giant. It grew and developed into a position of impact, which caused it to be distinctively different from those surrounding it.

Freemasonry took its terminological function from the early cathedral builders from which it probably arose. But instead of building cathedrals of stone and mortar,

Freemasonry began to build cathedrals of the human soul and spirit, using not stone and mortar, but using man's hunger for knowledge, truth and goodness, a love of God, and loyalty to his fellow man. And thus began our Masonic heritage.

As this potential giant evolved, it moved across the earth gaining in strength and influence, and created an effect which may be conservatively defined as enormous. We need only look back to its influence through its members on the impact it created in the development of the American nation for verification. During its existence, its influence increased and decreased at various times, but it was always felt. Based upon the result, there can be no doubt that it did indeed evolve into a giant. But make no mistake, it was its influence that made it a giant. Now, today, there are many leaders who refer to it as a sleeping giant. Definitely, a great potential little felt.

If Freemasonry is a sleeping giant and if indeed we do recognize its significance, it is time for us to awaken the giant lest we permit it to sleep too long and thus like Rip van Winkle find it awakens with an inability to achieve further greatness.

We must first of all comprehend why it is sleeping. We were a viable force throughout many generations of society. Why should we be less so today? Our philosophy has not changed over our years of existence; only the membership has changed. Have we become an anachronism in present-day society? Have our principles and values actually had no place for the last quarter century?

There can be no question that the environment has changed, and we must now determine whether we wish to retain our principles and values and lift others up to us or change to fit in today's environment, and thus step down to meet present-day standards. If we truly believe in the philosophy upon which we were founded, and upon which we existed for over 300 years, the decision is a simple one. Now we must determine our next move.

First, our future must build upon accomplishments of the present, not only to those of the past. We cannot continue to look back and dwell upon our past, glorying in what was, nor can we continue to mourn the loss. Pride in our past can be self-destructive if it causes us to ignore the present upon which our future depends. Longfellow wrote, "Look not mournfully to the past; it comes not back again."

My brothers, the potential to waken what we have chosen to term a sleeping giant, albeit an influential sleeping giant, is in our hands. We as individuals cannot pass the responsibility off to either the future or the present leaders. Each one of us has an obligation to the past, of which we are so proud. Longfellow also wrote, "Wisely improve the present; it is thine."

A great starting place would be to reinforce the Brother part of Brotherhood. I am firmly convinced it is of paramount importance that the practice of the Brotherhood we preach be restored to the Craft. We seem to have largely forgotten this fundamental principle which came so readily to our past brothers.

If the giant sleeps too long, it may change from a sleeping giant to a dying giant. I once read where Freemasonry was in a rut, and it would behoove us to remember that the only difference between a rut and a grave is the depth of the hole. My brothers, Freemasonry is too important to sleep, and is certainly too important to die. But we are the only ones who can awaken it.

[31]

Considering Success or Failure

For a good many years, I have given thought to the significance of Freemasonry, as well as the purpose of the Craft. Certainly, there are many definitions existing that state its purpose, all of them admirable, some ethereal.

There is no doubt that in many cases, and probably most, we succeed. In others, we fail. The successes and failures depend upon our efforts and systems, as well as our members' willingness to receive and respond to our efforts.

The success or failure of a man in life, however, depends more upon the recipient than upon the giver, and I would suspect that our failures are less of our making than of the brothers' willingness to accept our philosophies and principles.

I was reading the publication of the Grand Lodge of Hawaii recently and I saw a little quotation which impressed me. It was an old Indian saying: "When you were born, you cried and the world rejoiced. Live your life in such a manner that when you die, the world cries and you rejoice."

So great would be the Craft if we simply accomplished instilling that adage into our members. I have expressed a number of times that the value of the life of a man might be determined by the number who are sad when he passes away. That, basically, is what is expressed in the old Indian saying.

Our definition is to take good men and make them better. How much better could we do than to have the world cry when we die?

[32]

Let's Use the Freedom We Have

We have just passed through that period of the year when each of us probably pauses and considers the significance of the blessings and privileges we have been granted in life. It does not matter what our religious persuasion may be. It is a time when the existence of a Supreme Being probably carries a greater impact upon our hearts because it is a time in which our minds are stimulated more frequently to appreciate His importance in our lives.

We, as both Americans and Freemasons, have a greater reason to be thankful than perhaps those anyone else in the world. We live in a country were freedom is an accepted aspect of life. We live in a country where we can choose openly to worship God as we please, without concern. We live in a country where we can be a member of the Masonic fraternity without fear of any type of retribution.

And, yet we all too often take these freedoms for granted. There are many places in the world today where these freedoms simply do not exist. How often we tend to forget that our freedom to worship God, and our freedom to be a Freemason are freedoms earned by the sacrifices made by others. Prosperity has a way of dulling appreciation for those whose sacrifices and commitments gave us that prosperity. It is easy to become complacent when we have not had to struggle, and we have become complacent.

I have had the privilege in recent years to be in conversations with Freemasons from many parts of the world. As a result, I have developed an even greater appreciation for being able to walk into a lodge room and sit with my brothers, and of being able to walk into a church of my choice and worship God as I choose.

I have talked with brothers who had to leave their native countries because Freemasons were being persecuted and killed. I have talked to those who today live with a continuing concern for their lives or their freedom because they were Freemasons. I have written to brothers in countries where I had to use envelopes with no Masonic reference because it would place them in jeopardy.

And we, with no reason to fear, do not even put forth the effort to attend our meetings. We have so much for which we should give thanks to the Grand Architect of the Universe and to those who made the supreme sacrifice for our freedoms. We cannot do that by not using these freedoms.

My brothers, let us individually commit ourselves to make use of that which we have, the least of which is not the freedom of sitting in a lodge room with our brothers.

[33]

We Need Active and Passive Leaders

One of the great contributions that our Fraternity has made to the world has been in the area the development of leaders. We have been able to take men with potential, but with limited skills, and transform them from a relatively shy introvert or an untrained extrovert to become dynamic leaders of the Craft on all levels. They then carried this leadership ability to the world outside the Craft. Think how often you have observed members of your Lodge begin progression through the chairs and watch them improve in their capabilities prior to completing their terms as Worshipful Master.

Today, we are recognizing a lack of qualified leaders to guide our Craft. Why? Are we failing to attract the potential? Or are we failing to transform the potential? Or both? Because of the significance of this contribution, however, it merits our concern.

Over the years, I have observed two significant types of leadership. First, there is the one whom we would recognize and regard as an active leader. He is the visible one, the one listed on programs as a leader. He is the one wearing the jewels of the Craft.

I have been afforded the privilege of personally knowing some of the great active Masonic leaders of our time. I will not attempt to name them for fear of overlooking those of equal talents and contributions. They are the ones whose names are most frequently related to our Craft and the ones who are receiving the most credit.

But, there is a second type—one who is frequently overlooked as a leader. He is the one whose name is not listed as an officer, but is always there to participate. He doesn't wear Jewels, but his presence is imperative to our success. Both have been significant in the development and existence of the Craft.

When I first joined Freemasonry, I met an older brother of the Lodge who exemplified a different type of leadership than that with which I was familiar. He never held an office of any kind of which I am aware. But, he served on every committee for which he was asked. He did not drive an automobile, but he rarely missed a meeting of any Masonic body to which he belonged. Frequently, that meant waiting for a bus to get him to a meeting and hoping to get a ride home. This older brother was as totally ego free as anyone I have ever met. He never asked for, nor sought, recognition, but he offered to help all who were in an active leadership role.

Was this old man a leader? He was, in my opinion, one of the great Masonic leaders I have known because he served as an example for others. He epitomized to me what is significant as a passive leader. He led simply by setting an admirable example. Without men like that my Brothers, there could be no men like we, who are regarded as leaders. Of what value would the greatest leader be if there were none like him to follow our lead?

Freemasonry today needs both active and passive leaders. We need to find those with the potential to lead either actively or passively. We need to continue to provide to the world the leaders we have developed within the enclaves of our Lodge rooms. We, therefore, must attract and develop the qualified leader. When we develop leaders, we serve not only the Craft, but we also serve the world. After all, is that not our intent?

[34]

There Must to Be a Message for Us

It has been my great privilege in recent years to visit Grand Lodges in different countries. There, I was able to see Freemasonry, as it is practiced in other areas of the world. The basic precepts and philosophies, of course, are universal in our Craft; but the modes of operation vary considerably. This is not only evident within the Lodges, but it is also reflected in the attitudes toward them among the respective societies in which they operate.

I found that in most jurisdictions, it can take several years to become a Master Mason, a time during which Masonic education is given to each candidate. The Assistant Grand Master, the National Grand Lodge of France told me that, even with this time requirement, their membership has averaged ten percent annual increase for the last decade.

It is significant that the financial cost to become a member in most countries is much higher than what we are accustomed to in North America, and the dues are considerably higher. The requirement to learn the ritual, the history and the meaning of the Craft is emphasized much more than we emphasize it. And, most important, in some jurisdictions, attendance at meetings is not an option.

I have been greatly impressed with what Freemasonry means to those members and the significance that it carries into society in general. It is more reminiscent of the Craft in society of Colonial America. There must be some message somewhere in there for us.

This is not to say that problems do not exist in other countries, but most are of a different nature than those we face. The members know much more about the Craft than do our members and they show a far greater appreciation for the privilege of being a Freemason. The respect generated outside of the Craft in many instances is more pronounced. This creates a different environment in which to work than the one we know.

On the opposite end of the acceptance spectrum are those jurisdictions where the Craft is repressed by various authorities, yet there remains those who are willing to take the risk to be Freemasons. Our individual appreciation and dedication pales in comparison to the brother in most other jurisdictions. We have no threat of restriction of our freedom to practice the Craft, yet our greatest problem is the inability to even get our brothers to attend meetings.

I am much impressed with most of the Grand Lodges I visited, especially with the attitude of brotherhood, which I experienced. There exists that feeling of camaraderie and brotherly love, that at one time must've been more of a part of us.

I am optimistic for the future of our Craft in those countries where it is emerging after years of suppression. They know what it was to be forced to live without it and subsequently, have developed a greater appreciation for it. We who have had no need to struggle to be Freemasons, unfortunately, have lost our understanding and appreciation of it.

I also believe a great future for the Craft exists on the African continent, where it just arising. Those brothers are discovering the idealism of Freemasonry and what it means. They have the opportunity to weave the principles and ideals of Craft Masonry into a new fabric, one that can be different and yet the same; one that can help lay the cornerstones of democratic thought as it did in so many nations.

That idealism—the foundation of Freemasonry which causes us to believe—is alive. Its influence is still being felt, because its purpose of making good men better remains a fundamental purpose. I wish there were a way of instilling it into more of our members who take it so much for granted.

[35]

When Toleration Is Practiced

For almost thirty years, I have been writing and speaking to both those within and outside of our Craft concerning the significance of Freemasonry. Those presentations were made to proponents of the fraternity, as well as to opponents.

It has not been difficult to discuss at length those proponents of the Craft, one reason being that so many of them have, or had, names which are so easily recognizable because of their positive contributions to the history of mankind.

Indeed, history is replete with their names. These are men who led their countries in the struggles for what are basically some of the philosophical precepts of Freemasonry and were included as the precepts of their respective countries. Those of liberty, freedom, and equality of man are probably best known to us. It takes little effort to become aware of them. We need only to read American history to become fully cognizant of their significance.

There is, however, one other fundamental precept which characterizes this organization more than any other, and establishes the Craft as a friend of those who accept the aforementioned precepts and as an enemy of those who do not. This precept is the need to practice toleration of others beliefs. This quality of the Craft probably created Freemasonry's greatest friends and its most ardent enemies.

I mentioned that history is replete with the names of Freemasons who let their countries to achieve what are the ideals of the Masonic fraternity. I have discussed a number of them in the past, and I do not think there is a member of the Craft today who is not acutely aware of at least a few of them.

It is significant that history is also replete with the names of other men whose names are just as well known, but who are were enemies of Freemasonry. They were enemies because they objected to Freemasonry's emphasis on the need for toleration as a human tradition. Most will recognize the names of Adolf Hitler, Benito Mussolini, Joseph Stalin Francisco Franco, and the Ayatollah Khomeini, amongst others. Each one was an avowed enemy to Freemasonry, as well as an avowed enemy to democracy, both proponents of free thought. Where toleration is practiced, the political philosophy of those men cannot survive.

Several months ago, there was a seminar conducted for the purpose of responding to criticism of the Craft by several religious leaders. One observation I made at the seminar which was strikingly evident was that the opposition to the Masonic fraternity by those men was based upon the same premise as those men I mentioned above. It was made very clear that toleration of others beliefs is not to be accepted by the minds of those religious leaders, who have positioned themselves to be enemies of our Craft. The emphasis we place upon this practice is an antithesis to their methodology. One of the most discouraging aspects of being a Masonic leader, today is the need to attempt to educate those in the field of religious leadership who find Freemasonry incompatible with their doctrine, when we know full well that we encourage member support of their religion, probably more than any existing organization on earth.

It is a tragic commentary that the enemies the Craft have been the world's greatest tyrants and some of the world's religious leaders, both antagonists of each other. It is probably even more tragic that they oppose us for the same reason-the philosophical principle that man should not only have the right to worship God, but also have the right to worship God as he sees fit. An observation I made when I wrote my first Masonic paper almost thirty years ago was that there was no religion in opposition to Freemasonry, but there are religious leaders in opposition to Freemasonry. I find no reason to change that observation.

The greatest contribution that we as individual Freemasons can make to our Craft along these lines is to let those leaders of religion to whom we look for guidance along theological lines know emphatically that our commitment to the Craft and its principles is not only compatible to God, but as an organization, it reinforces our responsibilities to our Supreme Being and to our place of worship. Each of us has a stake in the contribution.

[36]

The Masonic Spirit Must Live On

I have recently read a book entitled *Votaries of Honor* ("votaries" meaning devoted or ardent persons to a cause or ideal), which is essentially a history of the Grand Lodge of the Philippines. I have been aware of the major influence of Freemasonry, through our early leaders in the development of the United States of America and assumed that no other country has been impacted by Masonic precepts, any more than has our country. When reading this book, however, I became more acutely aware of the magnitude of the influence of the Craft in the development of the Philippines. I also became more aware of how much Freemasonry meant to those men influenced by its ideals.

Complacency and ignorance unfortunately, have dulled much of the respect for the Craft that it justly deserves in North America. This is probably the result of most of the present generations having lost the need to struggle to have what we have. For the Filipino, the time span is not that great when they were still struggling to gain the freedoms which we take for granted—practicing Freemasonry being one of those freedoms.

We point with pride to our past brothers who played an integral role in creating this magnificent country of ours, let me quote the first president of the Philippines, Emilio Aguinaido, to show how much the Craft meant to them: "The successful revolution of 1886, was Masonically inspired, Masonicallly led, and Masonically executed. And I venture to say, that the first Philippine Republic of which I was the humble president, was an achievement we owe largely to Masonry and the Masons." Speaking of the revolutionists, he added, "With God to illumine them, and Masonry to inspire them, they fought the battles of emancipation and won." What an inspirational statement from one who should know.

There are two observations that I made from this book amongst many which should be foundation stones of the Craft wherever it exists. The first referencing the Craft that is: "Peace and harmony prevailed in the Fraternity. Men of different races, nationalities, religions, and political beliefs mingled together in the spirit of true brotherhood." The second relating to the occupation during the war stated: "It was only the outward manifestations of Masonry—the conduct of meetings and the holding of ceremonies—which the Japanese succeeded in disrupting. The Masonic Spirit, the very essence of Masonry continued to live on, in the hearts and minds of Masons."

Freemasonry in the world today has its greatest appreciation where struggle is continuing; i.e., the emerging former communist-dominated and third world countries. It always has been at its strongest when adversity has been at its strongest. Perhaps the strength lies in direct proportion to the challenges. Perhaps this is what is needed in North American lodges to strengthen them today. If complacency can weaken it, challenge should strengthen it. If the challenge does not come from without, then it must be provided from within, and realistically, it is already here. Apathy is just as prevalent within the Craft as it is outside of it. We are as guilty of taking Freemasonry for granted as are those outside of it in taking for granted all that we do for serving mankind. Indeed, that attitude may be the major cause of our decline in numbers.

Those of us, who are leaders must shoulder the respon-sibility to accept the challenge, to strengthen the Craft, to regain its influence, to retain its quality, and to destroy the apathy. We owe it to our past brethren and to the world. Our goal must be to reinforce those two foundation stones observed in *Votaries of Honor*. Peace and harmony must prevail, and the Masonic Spirit must live on.

[37]

Brotherly Love:
Give It and Receive It

Most of us as Masons are aware, at least to some extent, of the importance of Freemasonry to the development of civil society. This organization has made considerable contributions to the world benefiting many outside the fraternity. I wonder, however, how many of us truly appreciate how much our Craft can mean to the individual Mason. Due to your membership, my brothers, there are few places in the free world where you can travel today that you will not have friends. There are so many doors open to you because you are a member of the Craft; and yet, I suspect that there are very few who truly appreciate that aspect of membership. I am well aware that we do not join the fraternity for what we will receive from it; but there is nothing wrong in recognizing what the true concept of brotherly love is in opening ourselves to receive it.

I have been extremely fortunate in having the opportunities to experience this feeling of brotherhood beyond those that most members will ever have. It is there for all, yet few accept it. Regrettably, also in recent years, too few extend it. It is this expression of brotherly love to one another that probably has meant more to me than any other aspect of Freemasonry. To the world and to society in general, the Craft offers an ethical and moral basis of principles by which it guides its members. To the individual member, this fraternity offers an opportunity to express a feeling rarely known outside of it.

I recently returned from the Conference of Grand Secretaries held in Honolulu. There, once again, I had the privilege of experiencing the true feeling of Masonic brotherhood from Grand Officers from around the world when I announced to the conference, my intent to retire as an active Grand Secretary. It was an experience that I will never forget. I wish there were a way of transfusing into each of you that feeling, because I am convinced that should you know it, it would change your life in respect to your commitment to the Craft.

All of us are aware today of the declining numbers on the membership roles of Freemasonry. This loss in numbers has been impressed upon us for well over a decade and we look with regret that men of society today fail to show the interest in an organization such as ours. My greatest sadness, however, is not directed to our loss in members, but to the failure of the numbers that we do have to direct the feeling of brotherhood to each other. As Grand Secretary, I have listened to countless stories from brothers who were ill, or from widows of our brothers, who want nothing more than a compassionate contact with a brother. I would like to ask the question of them, when they were able, how much they offered, but I don't. Someday, my brothers, that may be all we want.

If we could recapture that quality which so greatly characterized the Craft in early America, it probably would go a long way toward reversing or decline in numbers. I encourage you to give and receive what is perhaps the greatest advantage of being a Freemason—the feeling of truly being a brother experiencing brotherly love.

[38]

Universal Brotherhood:
That Is Freemasonry!

You will recall the quotation from our ritual stating that "Freemasonry has endured the moral test of ages." This is a great credit to our Craft which few organizations can claim. But, Freemasonry has done more—much, much more—than having endured during those ages. One thing it has done is spread around the world. Almost everywhere that freedom exists, and even in some areas where it does not, Freemasonry may be found.

In a world of changing values, in a world wracked with tensions, wars and threats of wars, in a world where spiritual values and ethics are declining, there has been for several hundred years a bright and shining constant—Freemasonry.

Oh, maybe our membership figures are not shining as brightly as they once did, but our philosophy is... our purpose is... our goal is... our very reason for existing is still shining and it has not diminished one iota. The basic precepts of the fraternity today are as they were in 1717 when we had our structural origin.

Perhaps it would behoove us to examine more fully those precepts which have led to our longevity and a worldwide distribution. Why do we continue to survive when so many other organizations have failed?

It is my feeling that the primary factor affecting our success is inherent in the very foundation of our admission process. That single requirement of a belief in God, and not in any specific theology has been primary. This character provides a means of promoting a form of brotherhood that no single theology could ever hope to provide. It is the reason for the universality of our fraternity. There are those who have a problem with this philosophical precept and condemn us for it, but it is a universal foundation stone of our Craft.

There is no doubt that differences exist in Freemasonry around the world. There are differences existing in Freemasonry, even within this country; but it is the similarities, not the differences, which make Freemasonry what it is. The universal feeling of brotherhood from Grand Lodges around the world is impressive.

I had the great privilege of sitting recently in a subordinate Lodge in Mali, Africa, where almost all the members present were of the Muslim faith and where a Tuareg was being made a Mason. The feeling of brotherhood, which permeated that Hall was as universal as any I have experienced anywhere else in the world. This, my brothers is Freemasonry.

Our Craft seems to have retained this character of brotherhood in some areas, more than in others, but perhaps the need is greater there. The principles upon which it was founded do not vary, however. They are as old as civilization, itself: unchanged and unchanging.

We are part of the fortunate few, the relatively small percentage, who have had the opportunity and privilege to be Freemasons. Dr. Norman Vincent Peale, the great theologian, expressed his membership this way: "Outside of my relationship to the church of Almighty God, this is a most valued friendship of my entire experience."

My brothers, I continue to encourage you to become more cognizant of this great experience, more aware of the influence and significance of the Craft and more thankful that this is a privilege that has been afforded you. Then, and only then, will you truly appreciate it.

[39]

We Are Needed in the World Today

Many of our members find one of the most difficult tasks to be defining Freemasonry to the world outside of the fraternity in terms that they can understand. Over the years there have been many attempts to define it-some in very simple terms, others, in flowering phrases. Let us take a look at some of them and see what they tell us.

Freemasonry, has been defined as "the world's largest, most prestigious, and most widely known. fraternal organization" and as "a natural community of equals bound by shared experience and interest and united in action." Both of these definitions fit well into describing the Craft; but do they tell those who ask what it truly is?

There are other definitions that are more frequently used and less understandable by those outside of the Craft. The most definitive: "An organization to make good men better." The greatest reflecting our philosophy: "A Brotherhood of Man under the Fatherhood of God." The most glamorous: "A way of life."

I doubt if we used any or all of these definitions that it would suffice for any but ourselves to understand us and frankly, I doubt whether many of us would. For most of us, it seems easier to define what we are not, rather than what we are—e.g., we are not a political organization, we don't even permit discussion of politics in the Lodge room. We are not a religion, which is another subject, not open for discussion in the Lodge room even though we probably promote the practice of religious belief, more than any other organization. We are not a charity—and yet, we probably are the most charitable organization in the world.

We call ourselves "speculative Masons," but I suspect that better than 50% of our members don't even know what being a "speculative Mason" means; and yet, this speculative fraternity of ours has created one of the greatest impacts this world has ever known. In its almost 300-year organized journey, its incredible influences became forever marked upon civil society.

The value of the lessons taught in Freemasonry, however, lies entirely in the thoughts and inspirations that they stimulate in the minds of those receiving them. The lessons do not change, only the recipients change. My brothers, Freemasonry is more than a group of men—it is an ideal. It has served as an attractive force for some of the greatest men this world has ever seen. It has honored its commitment to us; but have we truly honored our commitment to it?

I have heard in recent years, questions raised by those both inside and outside of the Craft concerning the relevancy of Freemasonry in the current world. Could there ever be a time when our philosophy would not be relevant? If we are slipping in influence, it is our fault, not that of the outside world. Maybe that world is not as receptive to us as it once was, but it does not influence our quality as an institution. That control was totally in our hands. Therefore, the destiny of Freemasonry is subject to the membership, as it always has been. We cannot continue to make excuses to justify our failures. We need to understand more fully, our purpose and minimize our failures.

There is no question that our present way of life has

deprived the Craft of much of the opportunity of doing the personal things that were the source of its major strength in the past; but our philosophy is eternally relevant. We represent a bastion of tolerance in an intolerant world. Our philosophy and purpose could very well serve as a foundation for world peace. Our only weak link is us.

A Roman Catholic priest and a member of the Fraternity said several years ago, "If it takes our gentle Fraternity to teach brotherly love and tolerance to the churches of the world, then so be it!" What a great testimony to the relevance of Freemasonry in today's world. We are not only relevant; we are needed by this intolerant world and so mote it always be.

[40]

While Making Good Men Better, Freemasonry Became the Greatest Philanthropic Organization

Although the initial objective of Freemasonry is lost in antiquity, it is probable that its purpose was to maintain the quality and character of the early stonemasons in Europe. With the acceptance of non-cooperative members, it took on a character for which it is now known. Today, its major objective is strikingly clear—take good men and make them better. In the process of accomplishing that objective, it has become the greatest philanthropic organization, the world is ever seen. It has been determined that Freemasonry in this country contributes more than $1.5 million per day to charitable causes.

Freemasonry is an organization which requires a belief in a Supreme Being, and in that sense, is religious in nature. It has no dogma, no creed, and offers no means to salvation. It encourages all of its members to worship God in accordance with the dictates of their own consciences.

Inasmuch as it provides an environment where men of all faiths and classes can gather and relate to one another as "brothers." It promotes a Brotherhood of Man under the Fatherhood of God, which is not achieved by theologies. Tolerance is the byword of Freemasonry, it is with logic, therefore, that were tyrants reign Freemasonry ceases to thrive, since where tyranny exists tolerance cannot.

This becomes evident when it is realized the some of the first steps taken by Hitler, Mussolini, Stalin, Franco, Khomeini, and other dictators, were to outlaw Freemasonry and to persecute and kill Freemasons. Likewise, it also is evidenced with the resurgence of Freemasonry in the last several years in Hungary, Czechoslovakia, Yugoslavia, Romania, Bulgaria, Russia and other formerly Soviet dominated countries.

The Lodge also provides a forum wherein members of different political persuasions can sit together, realizing that no political controversy will result in disunity, nor mar the harmony during the meeting. Indeed, two subjects which are never permitted to be discussed in the body of an open Lodge are religion and politics. Masonic philosophy, although encouraging its members to be religious, and politically interested, believes that both are rights of the individual and not debatable in a lodge.

It has been suggested that the concept of present-day democracy originated in the establishment of Freemasonry. At the time of its probable origin around the fifteenth century, classism was a way of life. Freemasonry provided an environment wherein men of all classes of society could sit in the Lodge room as equals. In its evolution over the centuries, these basic principles and values of the Craft became more developed and emphasized.

The Masonic fraternity, in addition to working to improve the moral and ethical quality of its members, also seeks to stimulate each member toward the acquisition of knowledge. We encourage our members to study in all fields of learning, especially the liberal arts, to increase effectually their mental proficiency.

Freemasonry emphasizes that no member is to neglect his obligations to God, country, or family for the sake of the Craft. In short, Freemasonry, looks for the God-fearing, patriotic and devoted family man with the hope that we can improve these qualities and at the same time that these men will perpetuate the principles of the Craft.

One of the great advantages of Masonic membership is to have the knowledge, that as Freemasons, we can travel anywhere in the Free World and meet with unknown friends (brothers) who possess the same values and principles as we.

It is reassuring to know that if aid is needed all we need to do is contact the Lodge or a Brother. In addition, it is comforting to be assured that if our families need help, Masonic principles require members to provide assistance wherever possible.

Today, the objectives of Freemasonry remain the same. It continues to require a belief in a Supreme Being. It expects a commitment to patriotic ideals of the country in which one lives and emphasizes the need to enforce those ideals. It encourages a commitment to high family values, stimulating our members to practice those values.

[41]

A Memorial Day Ceremony

This talk was given during a Memorial Day service held at the cemetery in Everett, Pennsylvania. My very best friend for most of my life was serving as chaplain at this service. He was out of the hospital for only three weeks following a cancerous kidney removal. It was to be the last time that we would be together in that capacity. He died shortly thereafter.

I wish to thank all of you for having me here with you today to take part in expressing our appreciation to those who gave so much for our freedom. This is almost like a completion of a lifecycle for me. Over 45 years ago, when I was a Boy Scout, I had a job each Memorial Day of collecting and placing flowers on the graves of the veterans buried in the cemetery in Shippensburg. Then I became in charge of that function for a number of years.

For most of a decade, as an Eagle Scout, I led the first division carrying the flag in the Memorial Day parade. We stopped in the center of town to drop a wreath into a stream and the veterans honor guard fired a salute to the memory of their departed comrades followed by the playing of taps. Then we marched on to the cemetery for the commemoratory speech and again, the firing of the salute and taps.

To this day, the image of that ceremony, the passing of our flag and the playing of taps raises a lump in my throat and brings tears to my eyes because I learned what they represent.

Also, participating each Memorial Day as chaplain was a thin, suave former Marine Corps chaplain in his naval uniform. That man became my best friend. Well, I am no longer the young Boy Scout but then he is no longer a young dashing, suave Marine. But, we are both here today together in a Memorial Day service for the first time in close to 45 years.

From that experience as a Boy Scout, I had ingrained into my being, a great respect for the veteran and for the meaning of Memorial Day. To this day, I never let a flag pass me by unacknowledged nor do I hear the national anthem played and ignored. I refuse to forget my debt to those who gave so much that I might speak here today.

My friends, we do not have the luxury to choose the conflict, not any more than those of the past. We may not always be right but no other nation has ever given a greater definition of the word, freedom. George Mardikian, an immigrant to America and a successful businessman wrote, "Probably only those who were not born here can fully appreciate what it really means to be an American."

Men and events were brought together in the 1700s that forever changed the direction of civilization and the meaning of the word freedom. From then on, Americans have died or offered to die to defend it. Daniel Webster expressed well, what we all should feel. "I was born an American, I will live an American and I intend to perform those duties incumbent upon me in that character to the end of my career. No man can suffer too much and no man can fall too soon, if he suffer or if he fall in the defense of the liberties and constitution of his country."

I pray to Almighty God that Americans never need again to defend these ideals. But, if we do, I pray for Americans like those whom we honor here today. I thank God that I am an American and I thank the Almighty for creating Americans like them.

[42]

You Are an Eagle

Given at an Eagle Court of Honor of the Boy Scouts of America.

What a great honor it is for me to stand in front of you today at a program to recognize those who have achieved the rank of Eagle Scout. I recall reading recently a book titled, Beyond the Ordinary. Of the hundreds of thousands of boys who will join this great organization, only 1% will achieve the rank of Eagle Scout. Each of you has already shown an inclination to rise above the ordinary simply by achieving this rank of Eagle. I congratulate you, you have now made yourselves part of the minority.

I have been fortunate in my life to have received a number of recognitions and honors but there is none that has carried the impact than that of having achieved Eagle Scout status.

There is so much that Scouting has taught me that it is difficult to pinpoint any specific one that is more important than the others, but perhaps the one that has served me most has been the importance of interrelationships with others. It taught me that it is easier to be a friend then a foe. My friends, we are not born with fear. We are not born with hate. These we must be taught; these we must learn and Scouting helps dispel these hates and fears.

Most of the problems of the world could be cured by

the adoption of the teachings of the Boy Scouts of America. All the principles and precepts and all the teachings of scouting prepare you to accept a man for what he is. It teaches us to learn to accept what others have to offer. This is why I have such a great respect for Scout leaders. I know beyond a shadow of a doubt that I stand here before you today because of Scout leaders of yesterday. Their guidance and leadership stimulated me to do more than what I thought I could do and to be more than what I thought I was. Scouting more than anything else in my life, made me what I am.

Scouting changed my whole life. It first gave me confidence, confidence in myself and confidence to try where I might otherwise not have. It taught me that I could achieve and that I could accomplish if I really wanted to. It prepared me to be in front of people and to speak. (This will be the fifth talk that I will give this week.) But most important of all, it taught me the meaning of the brotherhood of man.

We must always remember that there is no one that can not offer something. No one is so poor of a man that he does not know something that we do not know. And remember my friends, life is not only for the wealthy and influential, it is for everyone, for you, for me. What we make of it is up to us.

Permit life to be a challenge to you. It is too easy to be ordinary. You are young. The whole world awaits you. If I have one regret as a result of the influence of scouting on my life, it is that I can never live long enough to accomplish all that I would like to accomplish. I do envy you that your challenge is mostly in front of you.

We cannot take a step in our lives without the influence of others. We will be nothing more at any time than a reflection of the influence of others along with our modifications. The poet Markham expressed it well when he wrote: "There is a destiny that makes us brothers. None goes his way alone. All that we send into the lives of others comes back into our own."

So, my brother Eagles, will you go beyond the ordinary? It is just possible but it is up to you. Accept what scouting has to offer. Learn! Learn the meaning of the brotherhood of man and give to others in equal measure what others have given to you. Maybe, then just maybe, you may rise above the ordinary.

You are Eagle Scouts, my brothers. Now and forever and none can take that away from you. And now, you must live the rest of your life like one.

[43]

In Honor of the Vietnam Veteran

Given at the Vietnam Memorial in Philadelphia, Pennsylvania, along with General Westmorland.

My friends, it is a tremendous privilege for me to be present here tonight and to be given the opportunity of expressing my appreciation for those whose names appear on this wall and on all the memorials throughout the world.

I guess I always nurtured the dream that someday I would have the opportunity and privilege to serve my country and thereby generate the same respect from others that I felt for our veterans, but, for me, this was not to be. I do know that were it not for them, I would not stand here today. It was because of the men and women whose names appear on this wall and thousands like them who received their countries call, who accepted the privilege to serve and who showed the courage to fight and to die, that we all stand here today.

In all the wars that America has fought, it was those who accepted the call to duty, many of whom gave that last full measure of devotion that now gives me the privilege to honor them, in words.

Although I never came close to Vietnam, it had a profound effect upon my life. I was teaching in a college at the time and was forced to deal with the range of negative emotions that permeated the college campuses and I experienced the frustration of trying to instill in my students the need to support all of our service personnel who were giving their lives so that they might sit in my classes.

I will never forget counseling one of my students whose brother's name is on a similar wall in Washington, D.C. She was experiencing the emotional trauma caused by other students' stance. Finally, out of frustration with the attitude of the students, I quit the profession that I spent years preparing for and which I dearly loved.

I do not argue the right or wrong of war. War can never be right. I do not reason its morality or immorality. It can never be the moral answer. But, it was there and our men were dying. War has been around since man first disagreed with man and we are in no position to judge the lack of a moral purpose of it when Americans are dying.

We must all, however, recognize and acknowledge that without those willing to serve and indeed to die to defend our freedom there can be no freedom. Without this willingness there can be no tomorrow. Indeed, without it there could not have been a today. Every one of us who is standing here today is doing so because of the men and women who were willing to risk having their name on a memorial like this one. My love and respect for them will never die. Your love and respect for them should never die.

There are 642 names on this wall, more than from any other metropolitan area in the United States. My prayer for all of us and for our country is that never again will the need for a monument like this occur. But, if it does, God grant that there will always be those Americans with a commitment and the courage like those whose names appear on this wall.

[44]

To the Honor of Those Who Served

Given on Veterans' Day.

Back in the mid-1700s, a fledgling nation was developing. In its embryological development, it developed a set of principles to support a different philosophy. This nation survived to become what we know today as the United States of America.

At the same time and developing parallel with this nation was a group of people setting those principles and establishing that philosophy. They also survived and are known today as Americans.

Both are here today because from that time until the present there have always been, when needed, a dedicated group of those Americans who were willing to give all that was required of them to keep America and Americans free. From the Revolutionary War to the Persian Gulf and now in Somalia, these Americans gave. Many gave all that they could give.

To have these principles and this philosophy, America was out of necessity born in conflict and to retain them has been tempered in conflict. My friends, there is nothing glorious about war but if it is necessary to remain free, if it is a requirement in order to retain these principles and that philosophy that was born in the 1700s, then we must be eternally grateful to those whose names appear on this memorial and similar monuments, and on grave markers and tombstones as well as to those who lie in unmarked locations around the globe. We must also pay this debt of gratitude to those who did return. For although their requirement may not have been as great, their willingness to serve was nonetheless an evident commitment..

No my friends, war is never glorious. It is never the moral answer. It can never be the right way. But, there are times because of tyranny and oppression that it may be the only way, and when this occurs, we as Americans owe to our country and to all past generations, our willingness to defend the legacy forged for us. We can never choose that conflict which we feel is right and ignore that which we feel as being wrong to be willing to support America.

We may not always be right, but we are the greatest nation on earth. There is no other that has given any greater concept of freedom than has the United States of America. If we are not prepared to give as those whose names appear here, we have the option to leave. There is no requirement to be an American.

I pray to Almighty God that Americans never need defend these principles again, nor this philosophy. But if we do, I pray for Americans like those whose names are here inscribed. I thank God that I am an American, and I thank him for creating Americans like them.

[About the Author]

Right Worshipful Brother Thomas W. Jackson is an eminent Freemason, recognized around the world for his work encouraging and supporting the Masonic fraternity. Bro. Jackson was made a Mason in Cumberland Valley Lodge № 315 of Shippensburg, Pennsylvania, and served as its Worshipful Master in 1969. He went on to serve a twenty year tenure as the Grand Secretary of the Right Worshipful Grand Lodge of Free and Accepted Masons of Pennsylvania, retiring in 1999.

He was also the first Executive Secretary of the World Conference of Regular Masonic Grand Lodges from 1998 to 2014, and is now Honorary President ad Vitam of that organization.

R.W. Bro. Jackson is a strong supporter of Masonic education and research, serving as the Warrant Master of the Pennsylvania Lodge of Research, a Fellow of the Philalethes Society, and a member of the exclusive Society of Blue Friars.

He has also held leadership positions in many other organizations concerned with the culture of the Craft, including the Conference of Grand Secretaries of North America, Masonic Information Center of North America, the Masonic Restoration Foundation, and the Association of Masonic Arts.

He holds honorary membership in thirty-nine grand lodges in the world, with Honorary Grand Rank in twenty, including Honorary Grand Master in twelve jurisdictions.

www.ingramcontent.com/pod-product-compliance
Lightning Source LLC
Chambersburg PA
CBHW032114280326
41933CB00009B/843